A catalogue record for this
work is available from the
National Library of Australia

NATIONAL
LIBRARY
OF AUSTRALIA

Hard cover edition ISBN 9780645030914

www.ponderings.com.au

WELCOME

Twenty Twenty was the year of stories. Our children will tell their children and grandchildren these stories for many moons, and the impact on our world will reverberate for many seasons.

During this spectacularly unusual year, we had the honour of interviewing and gleaning introspect from some wonderful people. The distance for many has bought about new ideas, reflections and most certainly that old sidestepping manoeuvre I like so much; allowing for pondering on a remarkable scale. We wear layers of these experiences like coats; the stories we are told form new paths. Sometimes the fibres have etched into our skin and the narrative finds new form.

Thank you for buying this book. Your support is part of the fibre of Ponderings; you are part of the mission to keep the thread of positive storytelling alive. Ponderings is an ideal of hope. We are grassroots, and whilst we are humble, far from perfect, we are most certainly human with passionate hearts. Ponderings is the stories of those we admire and who have helped us reflect, be inspired or prosper.

Our promise to our readers is to not polish and spin the original tale to make it more palatable or flashy. These are real stories and insights. The ones we might enjoy around a fire on a cosy night, or the beach at sunrise with a friend. We seek no prize or reward; only the pleasure of seeing these stories find their way to you like a message in a bottle.

Blessings to you and yours –

KIRSTEN MACDONALD
The curator of stories

We acknowledge the people of the Kulin Nation, on whose unceded sovereign land we work. We pay our respects to their Elders, past, present and emerging. We support the Uluru Statement of the Heart.

SUBSCRIPTIONS:
WWW.PONDERINGS.COM.AU/SUBSCRIBE

Ponderings

P.O. Box 353
Leopold Vic 3224
editor@ponderings.com.au
media@ponderings.com.au

EDITORIAL

KIRSTEN MACDONALD
Editor-In-Chief

KATE O'DONNELL
Operations Editor

CASSIDY KRYGGER
Writer, Digital Media

MONTANNA MACDONALD
Journalist

RENAE FAILLA
Journalist

CONTRIBUTORS

Janelle McMillan
Karen Brooks
Melissa Griffiths
Julia Lorent
Katie Moore

PonderingsMag

PonderingsMagazine

ponderingsmagazine

PonderingsAustralia

Ponder with us

For those who ponder

xx

WHEREFORE ART THOU DRAG KWEEN?

WRITTEN BY KIRSTEN MACDONALD

PHOTO PROVIDED BY ART SIMONE

Like pink chilled lemonade on a hot day;
Art Simone is fabuleux.

A dazzling Drag artist, entertainer, producer, star, gender illusionist, and makeup expert; Art Simone is an extraordinary talent. When we sat at our monthly Ponderings brainstorm and asked who do we want to interview the suggestion of Art Simone resulted in squeals of delight and so much enthusiasm you could bottle it and sell it at Milan Fashion Week.

Her website is a viewing platform of sparkle, and there is even merch in the online store. Would you like some success with that Boa baby? Art's guest role on the Bachelor filled the hearts of viewers; as she imparted words of wisdom about the strength in owning and embracing the gorgeousness inside and out.

When did you first try on a pair of heels, and what was that experience like?

I remember strutting in heels from dress-up boxes from a very early age, but the time I remember clearly was when I purchased my first pair of heels from an op shop when I was in high school - I was completely shocked to find a size 13 pair that fit my big old feet and snapped them up right away. I felt fabulous! And would wear them around the house so I could practice in them and enjoy being a lovely leggy lady!

Treehouse or Cubbyhouse?

CUBBHOUSE!

Feather or sequin if you had to choose?

Neither! Glitter all the way.

What makes the most fabulous drag queen?

To me, a fabulous Drag artist is someone confident and proud of who they are and what they bring to stage. When you're feeling the fantasy, the rest of the room does too!

What do you least like about the Entertainment industry?

The Majority of Drag Performers are self-employed artists, so we don't get annual leave, sick pay or super contributions – But hey, we wouldn't have it any other way!

What do you love most about the Entertainment industry?

Making people happy!

Is there a Drag Queen Etiquette and what would be the top 3?

Don't call us by our birth name

Don't touch us without permission (this includes our wigs, costumes and props)

If you're in the front row, please watch the show and pay attention!

Do you have a favourite relaxation destination, or do you prefer adventure and bustle?

I wouldn't be able to tell you the last time I travelled to relax, that just sounds stressful! When I need to chill out, I just love being at home – it's my nest and my happy place to rest, recharge and surrounded by comfort!

What is something most people would not know about you?

I have a third nipple– ain't that neat?

We loved your fave looks – very Jane Austen-esque are you a fan of old-world fashion?

My inspirations come from everywhere and anywhere, and we do love to pay tribute to vintage designs and inspirations. Everything old is new again, so we love to take these designs and give them a modern or sometimes futuristic makeover.

What concerns you about the world?

This list would be too long - instead, I see myself as a court jester, here to entertain and bring joy to the world so that we can forget about the negatives for a moment.

If you could give your 21-year-old self one piece of advice, what would it be?

I'm only 27, so I can't say my mindset is much different – I'm really proud of the journey I've taken and where I am now. Perhaps I'd say – keep doing what you're doing; you're doing great sweetie!

Favourite thing to do on a Sunday afternoon?

The Piano Bar Geelong; singing!

You can find out more fabulousosity about Art here: www.artsimone.com

JANE BUNN INTERVIEW

A FORECAST OF CHARISMA AND NOT A PLAIN JANE IN SIGHT

By Kirsten Macdonald
Photocredit: Jane Bunn

Jane Bunn is one very popular lady, with a prime spot as Australia's beloved weather presenter and a feverish 40,000+ followers on Instagram and an App on the horizon; Jane is a bit of an enigma.

A glamazon and fashionista; she is a seriously educated Meteorologist and Atmospheric Scientist, and she really (really) knows her weather! Forget Gucci and Balenciaga, when this lady starts talking about negative and positive dipoles, the juicy clouds, the Southern Annular Mode and climate drivers; welcome to Australia's Nigella of weather.

Warm, sincere and with a disarming enthusiasm; we are going to admit it, we were charmed.

There is so much to talk to you about!
Your education in meteorology, journalism and atmospheric science are extensive. Penn State is really impressive, how did that come about?

Well, I was at Monash University. To start off actually, I was studying software engineering at RMIT. To be honest, I was not great at it, but I'm so glad I did the first year of that because I don't love it, but it's handy! Then I worked for a little bit and worked out what I actually wanted to do, I found that I was procrastinating with the jobs I was meant to be doing. I was looking at the weather, and so after a while, I thought: that's actually what I want to do. This is what is driving me, this is what I'm interested in.

I went back to Monash Uni and studied a Bachelor of Science. I majored in mathematics and atmospheric science.

The coolest bit was everyone was going over and doing a semester abroad. Everyone else went to Oklahoma to chase tornados.

The thing that first got me into the weather was when I went skiing for the first time. I fell in love with snow. Instead of chasing Tornados, I went to Penn State so I could live in the snow for six months!

What is your purpose?

My original reason for getting into the job that I have now was because I was working at the weather bureau. I did a graduate diploma in Meteorology with them. Then I was working as a forecaster. There are certain words you have to use, terminology.

So we'd get them all in the right order and around the right way and what we could say. Then "the media'- certain people in it, would change those words and then change the meaning completely. But a forecast of "fine and mostly sunny", what "fine" actually means in Australia is "it's dry."

It says nothing about the cloud, whether it's hot or it's cold it just means that it's not wet. So a forecast of "fine and mostly sunny"- that means that it is completely dry and there's lots of sunshine.

So this woman on the radio used to take that and think it was a little bit too long and shorten it to "mostly fine" she had changed the meaning of that completely she said it is "mostly dry." So I'd be like what?

We put some wet weather in there that I don't know about? (laughing) So just a little tiny thing like changing one word around like that has massive meaning, and so I went, that's it! I want to forecast the weather.

I also want to avoid the middleman, and I want to be able to get the right information out to as many people as I can. And so, that's what I'm all about!

You've been on our screens for a long time now. Have there ever been any self-doubt moments, especially in the media industry for you? And if so, what was your strategy for continuing to shine so brightly?

Oh thank you! What I think about is where we're living now. Could you imagine having done this 20, 30 years ago where there was no social media? And the only people you ran into were the only people you got feedback from, rather than where we live now -which is so social media based.

Part of my job is to get the message out to as many people as I can. So, I put things out on Instagram, I put something out on Facebook, I put it out on Twitter. But then, people now have a license to say whatever they like straight back at you and you see it. So, that's what's interesting about how we live now is the feedback you get from that.

It can be anything from gross sexual stuff which I just completely ignore and move on from or things about the way I look or how I did something or those sorts of things. Some of it can hurt when you read it.

What I end up doing is overtime, working out a strategy of how to actually live with that. Some of the things are; Don't look at social media before you go to sleep- because that's the last thing you want to see before you shut your eyes.

Also, don't be constantly looking at it. Control how often you go and look at these things. My rule is; if you've said something gross I'm not going to respond to you. But if you've asked a weather question, then yeah if I have the time absolutely I'd love to do that. If you've said something that isn't correct, then I'll come back to you and try and challenge you and help you grow and understand what these things actually mean.

It's actually quite pleasing to see how many people I've been able to do that with. Just a one on one basis back and forth. We've been back 10 times on Twitter, and by the end of it, I feel like the person's walked away with "Oh I actually get that now." Which is good!

If you have a devastating personal moment or event or just having a shocking day and you've got to get up on that screen. How do you transform into that space?

When I get up, literally the first thing I look at is what may have changed overnight and then any data that comes in. It takes me about an hour and a half every morning. My husband loves it!

Then you sit throughout the day, and you are weather watching. Checking the radar, monitoring the satellite, seeing if has this popped up when it was meant to? What is the temperature doing? Then you are planning what you are actually going to go out and say there.

CONT...

I had a colleague once and we weren't getting along. She walked into my room at 5 minutes to 6 one night and started yelling at me. It was quite difficult from that screaming match then at 6:02 to go back into weather mode. As soon as I step into my shoes in wardrobe, and they put the audio pack on, and makeup are doing your last checks- there is something about no matter what else is going on- your head is there. It's dark in there. There are lights only in the right spots, so it feels like you're in the wings of a stage - so you're on!

What I'm trying to do out there is make sure the right information is getting out to as many people as possible. I think my mind just shifts and goes back into the right gear.

Do you think when you get to 40, you start to realise that you can actually give yourself permission on who you invest your time with?

Yeah, I agree. I reckon there is something about turning 40.

When you've got the big 4 in front of the number that you are now it's like you kinda go "I don't have time for this crap anymore" and you actually feel ok saying that.

Saying no, I'm ok with that and I've already moved on rather than thinking about it when I go to sleep, and I think that's a great way to be! I just wish I had that a little while ago

So what are the attributes that you find in people that really resonate with you?

Hmmm. I'm not sure how to answer that. The thing that is immediately hopping into my head is all the people that I have interacted with recently that have rubbed me up the wrong way! (laughing)

When you think about that question, why do you like hanging out with these people? And why do you not like hanging out with those people sometimes?

Some of the people you are with, you really don't enjoy being around, it's hard work. Whereas when you find people that you actually love, how much better is that feeling?

And just everything sort of inside. I reckon I got a little bit of that last week. I MC'd the Saints AFLW launch- which was so exciting to be a part of. The first year that the Saints have a women's team and I got to meet all of the girls. I got to read out their name and number.

To meet all of these girls, and see how excited and ready and pumped they are just before this new season. That energy rubbed off on me in such a good way. So I think when you interact with positive people you can get so much done in your world too. It's beautiful.

Cubby house or Treehouse?

I had a cubby house built for us when we were kids, but my dad took so long to build it that by the time it was built we didn't fit in it anymore! Anyway, that became the spot where we stored all of the pool toys.

To find out more about the wonderfully talented Jane go to: www.janebunn.net

THE EVOLUTION OF DOGS

By Montanna Macdonald

I am sitting in the sun on the grass in a pandemic lockdown, looking into the puppy dog eyes of my three-month-old dog as she eagerly watches the tennis ball in my right hand.

She tilts her head like mine, mimics the movement of my arm following the ball, and with tail wagging and tongue out, she happily leaps like lighting to catch it.

I ponder the evolution of the dog. Have modern-day breeds always existed?

How in the world do I domesticate and train my dog? Is my dog a genius? Let's dive into the history of our intelligent, globally superior favourite pet.

What we do know is that your cute puppy was once a wolf. Dogs evolved from their canine ancestor, a Gray Wolf.

To date, scientists are baffled by the timeline where wolves merged into dogs and the art of domestication.

Dog fossils date back as far back as 20,000 to 40,000 years ago in the Neolithic Era, so our fur babies are Stone Age, a friendship that has lasted eons. In studies by Professor Dr Krishna Veeramah at Stony Brook University, ancient fossils of dogs in Germany were very similar to our modern European dogs, even many of the breeds we have today as pets.

DID OUR CAVEMAN ANCESTORS CUDDLE OUR FUR FRIENDS OF JOY AND PLAY FETCH WITH BONES?

Another interesting study by Brian Hare, Director of Duke University Canine Cognition Center found that wolves have domesticated themselves into dogs, changing not only their behaviour to survive as companions with humans but also their physical features.

This self-domestication process of changing eyebrows, floppy ears, splotchy coats, are all a visible byproduct of their "friendly" evolution from wolf to dog. This is evident in the study of domesticated foxes in Russia, who made themselves look adorable over time and pick up on human social cues.

Your dog was once a snarling member of a pack that radically altered its appearance and manner to quite literally become our best friend! Crazy right?

So next time your dog gives you that puppy dog look when they want your dinner, remember, they are purposely putting on that face to get what they want. Cute, but oh too easy to give in.
There is also a unique bond between dogs and humans; when they look at each other, equally both brains produce the chemical oxytocin, a hormone which is likened to maternal bonding and trust.

Dogs are the first animal proven to have this bond with humans, and one of the first animals to domesticate itself with humans, well before humans were herding sheep, cows, pigs and growing crops. It is a beautiful connection between human and dog, and incredible to know a little history; from wolf to friend.

Anselmus de bood
fecit.

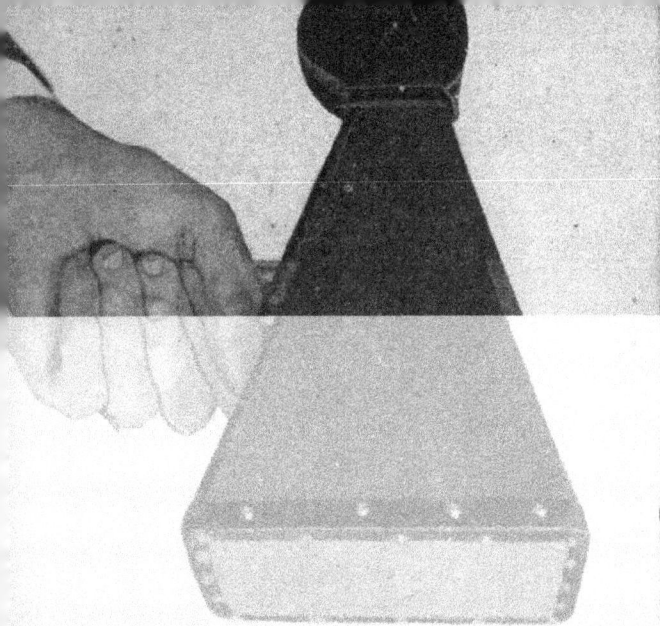

THE TANGIBLE OSCILLATION OF US

BY KIRSTEN MACDONALD

This earth spins, and its inhabitants live in a systemised structure designed to keep us animated.

Why? Perhaps to keep the axis infused with purpose. Functionalized pecking order is not reserved for the human species either; most species have hierarchical structures. From Zebrafish to Lemurs, many of earth's inhabitants distribute resources by way of categorising classes.

Birds and fish do not let their own starve, but then wolves will eat their young... there's that. It's the social stratification stuff that gets interesting. Samurai to Servant, Bourgeoisie to Butler, Brahmins to Shudras, we could go on for days. Words like **Third World, lower socio-economic, middle class, uneducated, academic, wealth, poverty,** powerful words all based around how products, food and energy is distributed.

Civilisation has transformed from tribes to towns and towns to towers. To feed the world, we are told we must control the soil, grow more, make the seeds more robust, use science to control the soil, so it absorbs the moisture, kills the bugs and then we kill the nutrients. So then we buy the supplements we need because the food does not give it to us. We try to stop starvation, and we swallow disease for the privilege.

There are even classes and equipment we can pay to do the exercise we would have done collecting water and making bricks or our growing food. A little ironic and chaotic don't you think?

But the uncanny thing is we can change the pattern, and we have everything at our fingertips. Physics tells us we can. Let's make a quantum leap here.

Life is a label we give to animated cells. Do we store our wisdom, our ancestral memory in our brain, our DNA, or in our ether or is it a binary system, a code written well before primordial sludge could swipe an EFTPOS card? Can existential lessons create a version of social inertial force? Imagine if we imbued these structures with a new form.

Have you ever heard of the theory of Spontaneous Self-Organisation? Universal and very complex phenomena are taking place in the physical, chemical and biological world, and it is science's way of understanding unexplainable order in the chaos.

Everything vibrates or moves; even inanimate objects are made of tiny particles. Here is where it gets interesting; when different vibrating forms are near each other; they will often get in sync with each other. Welcome to Spontaneous Self-Organisation.

An example is the patterned swimming of schools of fish, without any outside direction. When many fireflies get together, their light will begin to pulsate at the same rate. Crystallisation and snowflake patterns are another.

There are so many. Scientists are now working out how DNA does this, along with stem cells along with neuroplasticity. It's exciting, and it is complicated.

Magnets are an excellent example of SSO. Iron is a magnetic material and is made up of tiny magnets called 'spins.' Each spin will point in different directions, and their magnetic fields will cancel each other out. There is no order. If the temperature goes up, the more random. But when the temperature decreases, the spins will spontaneously align themselves, so that they all point in the same direction. Instead of cancelling each other, the different magnetic fields now add up, producing a strong overall field.

But here's the clincher, with spontaneous self-organisation there has to be disorder first for new random fluctuations to emerge. A dynamic state between order and chaos emerges otherwise called "The Edge of Chaos"

Only when chaos builds to a large point can a weak fluctuation be amplified to create a new pattern. If we are made of cells in animation, experiencing 'life" then surely we must be a 'life force."

When we endeavour can we align spontaneously with each other? What about consciousness? Is this a shared resonance? I don' t know about you, but there's a whole lot of chaos on planet earth right now. Is this life simulation or an echo bouncing back at us?

Is it not the stars that shine brightly do we reflect to them? Is this spontaneous self-organisation a science theory about to be proven, or is there a frequency of divinity that is not an external force understood of old but one mighty universe from within?

Wouldn't it be a cosmic kind of sonic bang if we aligned and were no longer controlled by genetically modified consumerism and started a new pattern? Fish swim, fireflies light. What if humans 'kinded?'

If every single action is committed with kindness, then maybe with a little physics, spin and a dash of positive loop feedback, we can evolve and change some of those class ideas while we are at it. We are like litmus paper; may we finally be ready to absorb the wisdom that comes in waves from our ancestors? Do we know how?

One can only ponder.

"FISH SWIM, FIREFLIES LIGHT. WHAT IF HUMANS 'KINDED?"

Dear Grownups

AN ODE TO PARENTS AND CHILDREN
BY
KIRSTEN MACDONALD

You are the humanity in which I am supposed to learn my way; teach me your wisdom. You have walked the path, burned the forests, surely you have the knowledge, you have discovered a way forward you might teach me or might help reduce my pain and heal my trauma?

For the trauma is supposed to be a lesson, not a prison. For the victim to become the warrior, will you hold the space with me?

Teach me?

Please don't outsource your love and transcendence. I have waited so long.

Don't you want to heal your heart while you help me heal mine? By the time I find these words, these big sounds you have taught me and I form them in ways to ask of you these things you have left. Your eyes glaze over, you have no time.

This thing called time creates a gap in the footpath I cannot jump over. This crack cannot be avoided, it is a fault line that isn't yours.

You are doing the best you can.
The only thing is I thought you had more. I was born with a promise you had more. More time, more love and calm. More peace and patience. I want.

Why was I born with this promise inside me? This expectation? It feels unkind, an empty box on a day of gifts. The guilt unfurls like ripped ribbon and I am starting to understand now. This is the way of things.

I shall snap these twigs between my thighs and start a fire, because you have taught me well and these things shall pass.

We shall stamp our feet on the earth, watch the dust fly up, saltwater, tear the leaves, sing into the wonder of night and laugh in the rebirth of the morning.

I shall love you, bathe your feet and know you as best I can. For the box was never empty, it was never a box at all, it was a message that said I am so tired my child.

"*I am no bird; and no net ensnares me: I am a free human being with an independent will.*"

CHARLOTTE BRONTE

M.Y.W.

THE NEGATIVE THINKERS GUIDE TO THE GALAXY

BY KIRSTEN MACDONALD

Warning: what you are about to read is a little bit of satire and irony, read if you dare!

ONE: Do you really need to talk about it? Wouldn't it be better if you bottled all of those traumas up that had nothing to do with you as a child and wait for them to manifest like potatoes sprouting out your ears? Tough people fester and pop with emotion later—a bit like a volcano burp only more dramatic. Hold onto it, if you dare.

TWO: Be a part of the problem; not the solution! Instead of wasting all that energy you have trying to understand a perspective different from yours; you could spend it coming up with a million reasons to defend an oppositional opinion that bears no assistance to anyone. So much less fun and helpful, and who wants to contribute in a positive way to society anyway? Geez.

THREE: Life only holds a certain amount of resources- surely there is not enough for everyone. If Jack has a better car than you do and makes more money but has the formal education of a gnat, it reinforces that adage- what's the point? No use developing your own unique path in life and finding abundance or prosperity. Jack has it all.

FOUR: You can't get what you want when you want it. You ask for it, and zilch. You have a plan, so why isn't it happening? Ask Veruca Salt; or Augustus Gloop. I want it now! Roald had a few thoughts on this; it ended with rotten eggs and getting stuck in a pipe. It could be worse. So plan wisely and expect the worst in your time frame you made up and told the universe to deliver. Giving the "universe" a deadline makes complete sense, don't you think?

the new world order is here

FIVE: Always be wary of politicians. No one ever grew up wanting to make a change in the world or aspired to stand up for the people. All snotty-nosed mean people just want to rule the whole planet, ruin it completely and get an excellent retirement package and make up taxes and legislation to make life difficult for everyone. We hear they have a secret handshake involving a pinky on the lip with a cackle. They eat criticism for breaky like cornflakes. Its a new world order.

SIX: Are addictions REALLY that bad? If you are a high functioning addict, what is the worst that can happen? You only live once right, except when you don't.

or is it?

SEVEN: Make sure you watch the news at LEAST three times a day. Get all the latest updates on your phone or any device you have. You must not miss a beat. That arrest in Brazil might impact the price of bricks in Tootgarook. Believe everything you watch, the world is a big bad place, and you must be on top of it, if not to think about but to cause you subconscious stress which is like salt and pepper for Number 5 and 6.

EIGHT: Self-doubt: doing this before anyone else can certainly keep out the go-between. Why buy wholesale when you can make it your self? Doubting yourself at every turn is a sure way to stop worrying about doing anything new or exciting; both emotions that can induce feelings of joy, so TREAD CAREFULLY HERE PEOPLE!

Discomedusae. — Scheibenquallen.

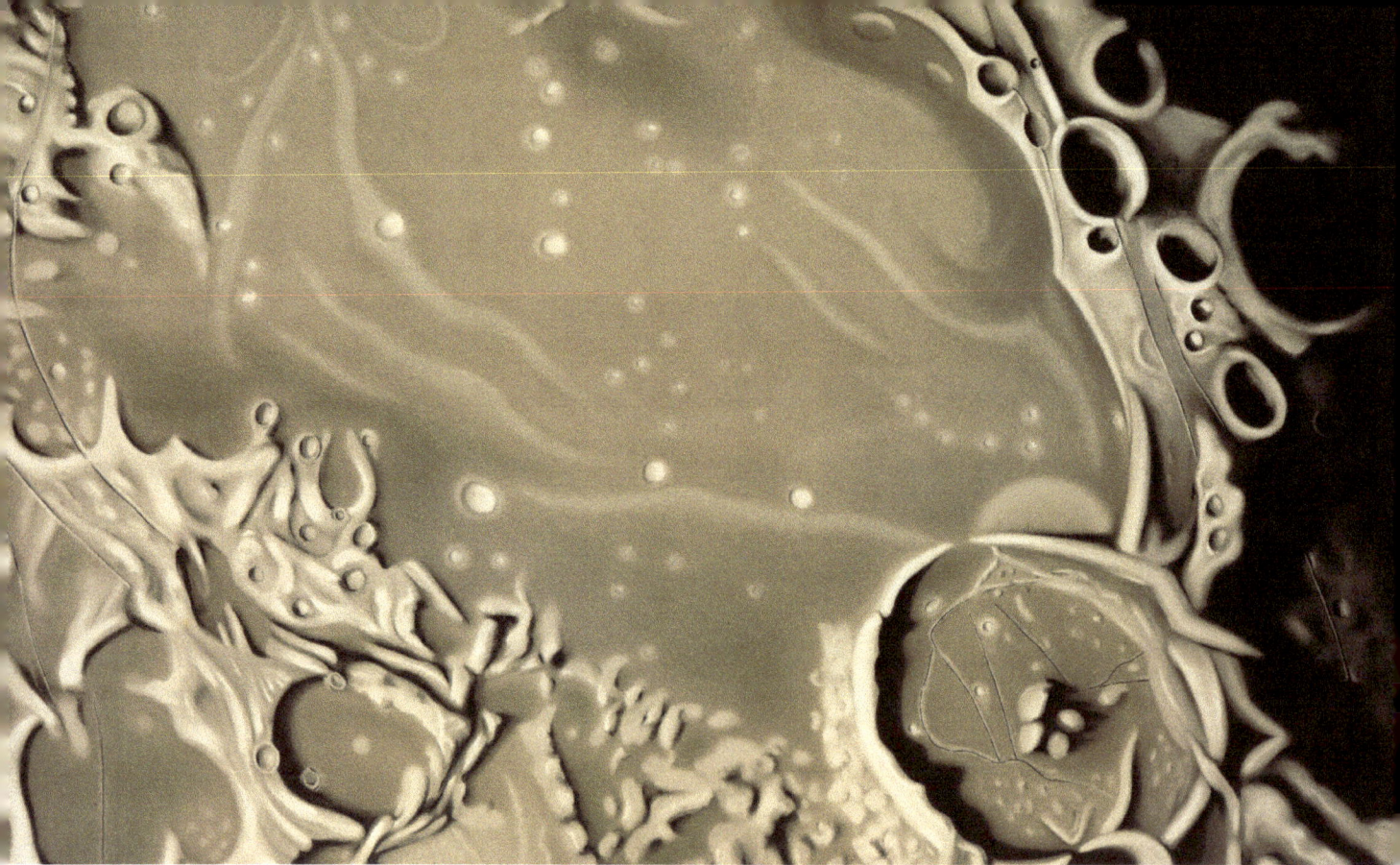

CONT...

NINE: Ruminate, ruminate and more rumination! Ruminate: mid 16th century: from Latin ruminat- 'chewed over', from the verb ruminari. To deeply think. Then get stuck ruminating. A hamster in a wheel springs to one's mind, and why not? It's not like your time can be spent doing something more constructive anyway. 10,000 mental steps in the reverse direction must be suitable for something surely.

TEN: Don't change. The only humans who like a change are babies. Change means different. Different is scary. Scary means no, right? Learning more about the world just makes life uncomfortable, undoubtedly it's much better to sit in the proverbial and endure? Endurance means a tough skill set, and if you pair this with bottling shit up, with a dash of self-doubt, a sprinkle of global suspicion and a ripper addiction you have my friends a brilliant cocktail called the Clusterf**k delight; shaken not stirred. It goes down a treat with a twist of impatience and a bowl of conspiracy theory.

End note: please be advised this is satire and a tongue in cheek reflection. If feeling overly negative, please seek professional guidance.
Lifeline: 13 1114

The only humans who like a change are babies. Change means different. Different is scary. Scary means no, right?

The Blazing Heart of Community

WORDS BY
Kirsten Macdonald

PHOTOS BY
Kate O'Donnell
BlazeAid Australia

Like many all over the world, our hearts are left swollen and aching as we witness on our screens and for some in their backyards; the scorched earth and hellish sky. Beach blue now engulfed with smoke haze and embers of the worst kind; scarring the land with unprecedented ferocity. Beneath with sooty tears and anger lies the desperation of people fighting in what has become one of the worst National disaster bushfires in Australian history. The devastation runs deep and will continue long after the last flame has sputtered out. For the impact of wildfire is a destructive force that will echo forever.

As we heard the stories from friends and family defending their homes, we felt desperately sad, angry and frustrated, helpless.

Our friends were left without water, listening to the cries of dying animals, burning fauna and drought-impacted earth baked to concrete under the glazing sear of intense heat. Lives were lost, people and wildlife, pets and livestock. Gone.

Started after Black Saturday in 2009 by Kilmore East farmers Rhonda and Kevin Butler, BlazeAid is volunteer based and has helped rebuild fences and lift the spirits of people who are often facing their second or third flood event after years of drought, or devastating losses through bushfires.

BlazeAid volunteers work in a disaster-affected area for many months, not only helping individuals and families but also helping rebuild the local communities.

The 100% Australian run registered charity currently has 14 base camps around Australia helping on the ground. So Kate and I packed the boot with goodies and made the trip to Lexton Victoria to meet with Bruce Hindson, co-ordinator of one of the camps. We drive on a dusty road into a popup township of campers, caravans and tents. We soon realise we are in good company, a thriving and bustling place. The trailers are lined up ready to go out for the next job, each one equipped with the tools needed to build fences and make repairs. But BlazeAid isn't just about fences.

As Bruce explains, it's really about people. *"Talking to people on the phone is okay, but actually dropping in and having a cup of tea, face to face can make all the difference. You have to meet people, shake their hand, check-in and listen. People underestimate what this means. When you have a team of people staying nearby at a hall, or a footy ground that are there to help you get back on your feet and get the fences mended, it can change everything for a person. Fences are expensive to replace, and people have sometimes had everything wiped out. You got no fences? You got no farm. To help them with an ear, a conversation and a sense of community go a long way."*

With trailers stationed in every state, BlazeAid has anything from 15 to 110 people turn up to help with a carefully planned roster, logistics and rebuilding set up. People may give 2 hours of their time or two months and the dedication of return folks each year gives you goosebumps. The Lions Club are there today, donating their time and helping set up a marquee tent for more room. Bruce and his wife Janice tell us the community generosity is fantastic. They tell us the story of one night everyone was at the local pub, the publican put on a special meals night at a discount price for all the BlazeAid crew. When they went to pay for their meals, 2 x locals had covered the lot.

"People look after each other, and there are so many more stories like this, it happens all the time," says Bruce.

BlazeAid.com

Fires   Floods
Cyclones   Droughts

"I am not going to lie to you, there have been times when we have rolled up, I have met a farmer and thought I would see him hanging from a tree by the end of the week; the devastation runs that deep. But what do you know, a week later the bloke and his family are smiling, they have some future to look to and feel a bit of support. That's what happens."

CONT...

People think once the fire or flood has gone, it's all over with. But this is not the case. It's like a funeral, at first the casseroles roll in, then 6 weeks later everyone starts to get on with their life. This is often when families are only just beginning to come to terms with what has happened and wondering how the hell they are going to get going again" says Hindson.

A sobering thought.

For many, they might not have lost their lives but may have 200 head of sheep badly burned, or wildlife living on the property, ancient trees protected on a generational property. Animals they have raised have died. Or perhaps they might have hundreds of acres of crops ruined, years of work gone in a moment. They may have already been suffering from drought, and this type of disaster is the straw to break the camel's back. Let's not forget sacred sites and the lands of native animals close to the country's heart and soul.

The team in the kitchen are working away and tell us there is a real "get this done" mentality along with lots of laughs and big smiles and you get the feeling this is a marathon, not a sprint.

An operation like BlazeAid costs anywhere up to $5000 a week for a camp to run and facilitate. Relying on volunteers, business sponsorship and the help of the donations from the public it is a 100% charity. It relies on these funds to help it continue to grow, engineer trailers and get on the road to having those conversations to those that need help the most. You can find out more at https://blazeaid.com.au.

The Monkey Brush

ARTIST EXTRAORDINAIRE

Interview with Debb Oliver – The Monkey Brush

By Renae Failla
Photos by Debb Oliver

Skyrocketing to fame only months ago, Debb Oliver has become somewhat of a household name in the Australian digital illustration industry after one illustration, in particular, was brought to the attention of a very famous family.

Debb modified the group photo of Chandler Powell, Bindi, mum Terri and brother Robert on Bindi's wedding day by adding their dog Piggy, her father the Crocodile Hunter Steve Irwin and his beloved dog Sui. Through social media and word of mouth, the family saw the heartwarming illustration in no time.

Originally from Brazil, Debb moved to Australia as a teenager and now resides in Sydney with her two boys and husband. Her personalised watercolour portraits are her speciality and almost every piece features nature, her second passion.

Tell us a bit more about the portrait of Bindi Irwin, her family and her late father Steve Irwin.

As I said, I have a diploma in Biology and I must say Steve and Terri were my biggest inspiration alongside Dr Jane Goodall. I cried for days when he passed, and I kept loving his family. I'm a huge animal lover, and the work they do is just unbelievable. When Bindi got married, I had this mix of emotions. I was so happy for her but so sad that Steve didn't get to walk her down the aisle. I decided to draw the portrait of her family on her wedding day and include Steve and Sui.

I posted on my social media, she saw it, thanked me, sent me gifts, made it her profile picture on Facebook, posted it on her social media and I flew to QLD to personally give it to her on her birthday. I met all the Irwins and they were more amazing then I could ever have imagined. The story was featured in 17 different papers and it's been the highlight of my career. Can't wait to draw them again when Bindi has her baby.

What inspired you to paint this portrait?

My immense love for them and the wonderful work they do.

Describe your encounter with the Irwin Family.

It was unbelievable. Due to COVID, we couldn't get too close to them, but Bindi kept saying she wished we could hug and I had to contain myself lol. I got to share that amazing experience with my two kids and they loved it as much as I did. It was incredibly special.

Where does the name 'The Monkey Brush' come from?

I worked at a childcare centre teaching arts. There was this beautiful boy called Ethan, who was so sweet and curious. At the time I was also studying biology and we would spend a long time outside naming every bug and plant. I told him possums loved eating the flower "bottle brush" and he loved hearing about how I'd collect them fresh every night for my rescued orphan baby possums. Every time he was cheeky, I'd affectionately call him monkey. And one day when he saw me, he asked me if I had found some "monkey brush" flowers for my possums. I thought it was the sweetest thing. I often wonder where he is in life, and when it came time to choose a business name, I thought of that special little boy.

What is your perfect day?
Good food, family, good music and a pretty summer sunset.

Describe 3 of your favourite pieces.

The Irwin portrait.

One called "to parish in paradise" where I illustrated how difficult but fulfilling motherhood is.

One called 'empty arms ' where I honour mothers who have lost babies or couldn't conceive. I lost 4 babies and it's a very important theme for me, and I'm glad I can use my art to bring some healing to others.

What advice would you give any budding artists out there who are either looking to start their own businesses or to have their artwork displayed in galleries?

Work hard, value your work, practice every single day, be kind to people and trust the process.

How old were you when you started drawing?

I can't remember. My mum is sure I came out of the womb holding a pencil. Lol

Is there anything else you would like our readers to know about you?

I'm firstly a mum, trying to juggle life, family, work, etc. I sleep 4 hours a night on average and I draw around 8-9 hours a day, and I still have to do admin and maintain social media.

I also have an autoimmune disease and fibromyalgia. People assume working with art is easy. It's not! It's hard, but I wouldn't have it any other way. I'm grateful for the support I receive, and the privilege of working with what I love.

To check out an array of Debb's inspiring artworks, head to her Instagram page @the_monkey_brush/

THE MAGIC OF BEES AND THE BEAUTY OF NUMBERS IN NATURE

Why do bees buzz? What does maths have to do with sunflowers and the many beautiful fractal patterns of our world?

A favourite book in our home held some wonderful clues to the mysteries of our hidden world. Critically acclaimed science-fiction author Ian Stewart is a British mathematician. He is Emeritus Professor of Mathematics at the University of Warwick, England. He has published more than 120 books, with an extensive list of impressive titles to wet your Harry Potteresque whistle.

Books such as Professor Stewart's Cabinet of Mathematical Curiosities, Why Beauty Is Truth: A History of Symmetry, How to Cut a Cake: And Other Mathematical Conundrums, Professor Stewart's Hoard of Mathematical Treasures and he even has an award-winning app, Incredible Numbers by Professor Ian Stewart. The Beauty of Numbers in Nature is Ian Stewart's preface to his masterpiece and a touching genesis.

CONT...

"When I was six, a friend showed me some curious little five-pointed stars that he had found on the beach...I became aware of a deep mystery: why does nature produce so many patterns?" - Ian Stewart

Stewart's language maintains the mystery in the metrical, but the plurality of simple explanations and anecdotes make for fascinating reading. A feast for the mind that is anything but mundane.

Many shapes in our world typically look flat-faced in geometry. Not the spiral.

"One of the favourite patterns of life, in fact, is based on curves- the spiral... Spiral shells appear way back in the fossil record, and one of the most common. The shell is formed by a soft bodied organism, for protection. As the creature's size increases with age, it outgrows its existing chamber and builds an extension into its house."

Chambers and hidden secrets. It is no wonder Sir Terry Pratchett awarded Stewart Honorary Wizard of the Unseen University.

He goes on-
"On land, snails build similar shells. Snail shells and indeed many seashells, often coil into the third dimension. Of course, the shape of the shells is always three dimensional: what I mean is that the "core of the spiral", the line that runs along the centre of the chambers, ceases to lie in a plane and starts to curl into a third dimension of space."

I will never step on a garden snail again. An architect of a logarithmic spiral, powering into itself - not all it seems in our microworld.

CONT...

Fibonacci, the son of a custom's officer, was a numbers man. His problem solving around rabbit populations in 1202 spawned mathematical patterns that would revolutionise thought. In basic terms; where after the first two numbers, each number is obtained by adding together the previous two numbers in the sequence. eg 1,1,2,3,5,8,13,21,34,55 – each number in the sequence is the sum of the previous two numbers.

Stewart observes:

"Fibonacci numerology and spiral geometry are surprisingly common. They suggest that plant growth obeys simple but subtle mathematical rules, which lie somewhere in the interface between dynamics, geometry and arithmetic... Fibonacci numbers have penetrated deep into the mathematical psyche as an apparent endless source of inspiration and wonder...these numbers occur in the spiral structures many use to arrange their seeds. Fir cones are a good example. The seedhead of a sunflower displays these spirals in a gloriously regular pattern. Lillies have 3 petals; buttercups have 5, delphiniums often have 8, corn marigolds have 13, asters have 21."

SILVER-LEAVED SUNFLOWER
(HELIANTHUS ARGOPHYLLUS)
$^2/_3$ Nat. size
PL. 139

Like your veggies? According to Stewart;

"The same numerology can also be seen in cauliflower...we find that the lumps are arrayed in beautiful spiral swirls. Sometimes the eye of a mathematician can see things that other eyes miss"

A golden angle is achieved with spiral growth which impacts things such a seed spacing, protection, growth and efficiency of survival. Ponderers we are consuming an intricate pattern of design, not just nutrients! The microcosmos in our backyards and onto our plates is extraordinary.

The Magic of Why A Bee Buzzes

"Most of what goes on when a creature flies is invisible to the eye because air is transparent. A bird in flight spins of a regular pattern of vortices, swirls of air spinning off from the trailing edges of its wings. The bird exploits these vortices to gain lift. Only recently have human engineers understood this particular trick, but the birds have known for a hundred million years...We know how bees and other insects pull off their counterintuitive feat."

"Their wings move upward until they almost touch. When they beat downward, the sharp edge creates a leading-edge vortex. For reasons we don't fully understand, this vortex remains 'stuck' to the top of the wing, generating lift, and spirals along it until it is shed at the wingtip. This method requires small wings that beat very rapidly, which is why bees buzz. And it's why the flying pig will remain a metaphor for the incredible."

Don't you wish we could see air in colour?

The Beauty of Numbers in Nature is 223 pages, explaining every pattern imaginable, cascading into a presentation of deep philosophical questions about the foundations of physical law, the nature of space, time and matter, and the shape and history of the universe. Order in chaos, time travel and the realms of understanding is more than enough to nibble on. With beautiful pictures, this is the perfect coffee table book and will have you pondering.

https://ianstewartjoat.weebly.com

"When nature keeps reusing the same catalogue of patterns, the wise scientist pays attention."

IAN STEWART

Five More Minutes

Words by Julia Lorent

My mother was amazing. When you look upon her life and what she was able to achieve it truly highlights something many people forget; adversity doesn't have to define you. She was strong but didn't really know it. With six children, including a daughter who was intellectually challenged, she needed to be.

Mum was a lot of fun and enjoyed a good laugh. Life was hard in our house, but because it was filled with so much love and laughter; these became sacred bonds- unbreakable. This family of mine is etched in humour and support; we are there for each other, we argue like hell, but we love each other very much. Interestingly, all of us have careers focussed on helping others. I believe this is a legacy my Mum would be very proud of.

Not many people I know have the relationship that we have; it often draws comment from those we know. It is 100% because of our parent's influence.

A football team of kids would be carted from sport to sport in the car, and if anyone was in need, my parents were the ones to help people out. Material possessions were of no importance. Tragedy smashed through our door uninvited at age 46 for my mother and our family when the love of her life (my dad) died.

With six children, no income, no life insurance and a broken heart; times were beyond tough. My mother was a strikingly beautiful lady; very Nigella-esque but without the sexy mannerisms. The next tragedy was the disconnection with her married friends. Husbands were hitting on her, and she became a perceived threat, she was often blamed. The womanhood did not support her.

These were all tragic events that saw her trying to be very strong and support six grieving children who lost their dad. It must have felt incredibly unfair. We all had our individual and collective issues about the sudden and unexpected loss of our father; totally overwhelming and insurmountable. She also had an intellectually challenged daughter who had bouts of intense violence and a system that echoed back with no help or answers whatsoever. There was just no help. Here was a woman trying to make sense of her own life, grief and heartache then depression while wondering the whole time what the hell she did to deserve it.

But somehow we got through it, not unscathed, but through. Even when we were at our lowest, our mother's love and support kept us together.

Her one true friend and companion were cigarettes; she thought they got her through; it was her time out, her thing. While she always had intentions of QUITTING, they too turned on her.

She was diagnosed with advanced Lung Cancer. She QUIT instantly, but it was too late. I try not to overthink about it because it fills me with sadness that when her friends should have been there for her, the only friend she could trust was her cigarettes. It is very sad and breaks my heart to this day.

> **When I see people flourish and live a beautiful life, full of authenticity and richness because of the work we have achieved together; it is the biggest reward I could ever ask for. The lives of those who love you are worth saving, not just your own.**

Cont...

We loved her deeply. We all ended up with a very strange sense of joint humour, which often bubbles up when tragedy strikes. It is what gets us through, and we have our parents to thank for this. Dark humour can be an excellent tool. I wish we recognized it at the time. I wish we told her more how damn strong she was, acknowledged her more and just had five more minutes. Only 5, how good would that be?

Little did I know that this would not be the only time I would be what I call the – Hidden Victims of Cigarettes. Anyone that has experienced the crippling anguish from losing a loved one knows how close it can come to derail your life.

Instead of letting my grief beat me, I decided to channel it into helping others fight their own demons.

For the next two decades, I would leave no stone unturned to find answers in helping people with addiction and practices, with no judgement.

For the judgement of others is too harsh a force to be reckoned with. The result has been a career forged in helping others, and it has been successful. I think people understand I don't judge and I have the skills to help them navigate a better life. I am the founder and principal practitioner for Melbourne Quit Smoking Clinic, Melbourne Clinic of Hypnotherapy, and The Savvy Changemaker. www.thesavvychangemaker.com

FOOD GLORIOUS FOOD – AUTISM AND EATING

by Kate O'Donnell

"HERE COMES THE AEROPLANE... OKAY, THE TRUCK? THE MERMAID?

JUST EAT IT!"

Sensory sensitivities can involve taste and smell. So when it comes to food, sometimes there can be little hurdles and sometimes epic ones. Often it comes back to the texture of the food in the mouth, which can create a gag reflex and vomiting.

Given that food is both necessary for nourishment and life, this is an important one to try and overcome if you can.

Food is also a very social event these days, so you have this impact as well. In our house, planning meals for a family of four felt like preparing three different meals for a royal family. One person eats only soft food, the other only likes crunchy and don't even think about mixing anything, or it's over before it begins. We can finally laugh now about the times we sat with Mister in his toy car to eat.

The number of times we have watched and played games on the iPad just so we could spoon-feed with distraction! And yes I can hear the criticism, but when the other option is a feeding tube in hospital you don't question the iPad! Sometimes you have to do what works.

CONT...

At times it felt mealtimes were like the story Green Eggs and Ham by Doctor Seuss... "Would you on a train, would you could you in a boat... and a whole lot of not in a boat, not with a goat, I will not eat there here nor there, I will not eat them anywhere. I will not eat them, Sam, I am I DO NOT LIKE GREEN EGGS AND HAM!" Insert tired, stressed parents, nutritional deficits and loads of worry.

Distractions are good, enticement, a reward system with the passion factor being used again. Trying to source some choices that can fit into your child's likes, whether that is smell, texture, shape or colour.

Go gently when introducing anything new, remember to use stories and habits. Never stop offering new foods. Food time should never become about a parent becoming angry or trying to 'make' the child eat.

This is a sure path to disaster.

Yet again you may be faced with comments from those gorgeous helpful 'others' like: "Picky eater, fussy, choosey, spoilt... just make them eat it... they need to learn...back in my day...if they are hungry they'll eat..." NO!
Planet Spectrum doesn't work this way! Please know that if food/eating is an issue for your child, you are not alone. Our family worked with the OT and speech pathologist... There are thirty- two steps to eating...Who knew?

We worked on playing with food, sensory issues, no stress at mealtimes, modelling, and the importance of still offering a variety of foods. There are so many different areas to eating and food that your OT and speech pathologist can work on with you.

TIP - If you are experiencing difficulty with your child's eating, limited food choices and mealtime disarray- you need to seek help from your OT and speech pathologist. This is their area of expertise! Head over to www.planetspectrum.com.au for Autism resources.

MAGGIE JONES OF CLE[...]

Exercise Myths, Activewear and Do You Want Coffee With That?

WORDS BY
Sarah Healy

Sarah Healy physiologist and columnist unpacks the myths about exercise and gets straight to the point!

Extra flexible people are double-jointed – Nope, not a thing in humans. Joints can be hypermobile, but there are definitely no extra joints in there! In fact, hypermobility features joints that easily move beyond the normal range expected for that particular joint, which can be very handy for the contortionist and party trick, but alas, not an extra joint in sight!

Running is bad for your knees – Research has found recreational runners have a lower risk of developing osteoarthritis than non-runners. Everything within reason, of course, as the studies also showed that runners training and competing at a very high level for more than 15 years have the same likelihood of developing osteoarthritis as the general population. If I were talented and dedicated enough to be able to compete at such a high level for so long, I'd be happy to take that risk.

You need to wear ACTIVEWEAR to exercise – Definitely not. Anything comfortable to move in will work. I've been known to get a few exercises done before breakfast in my PJ's, so no judgement from me! We know everyone loves a good lycra, but it's about movement not Lorna.

When you ride with a group you must stop for coffee – full disclosure, I used to ride in a bunch and more often than not we stopped for a coffee, but I'm just saying you don't have to.

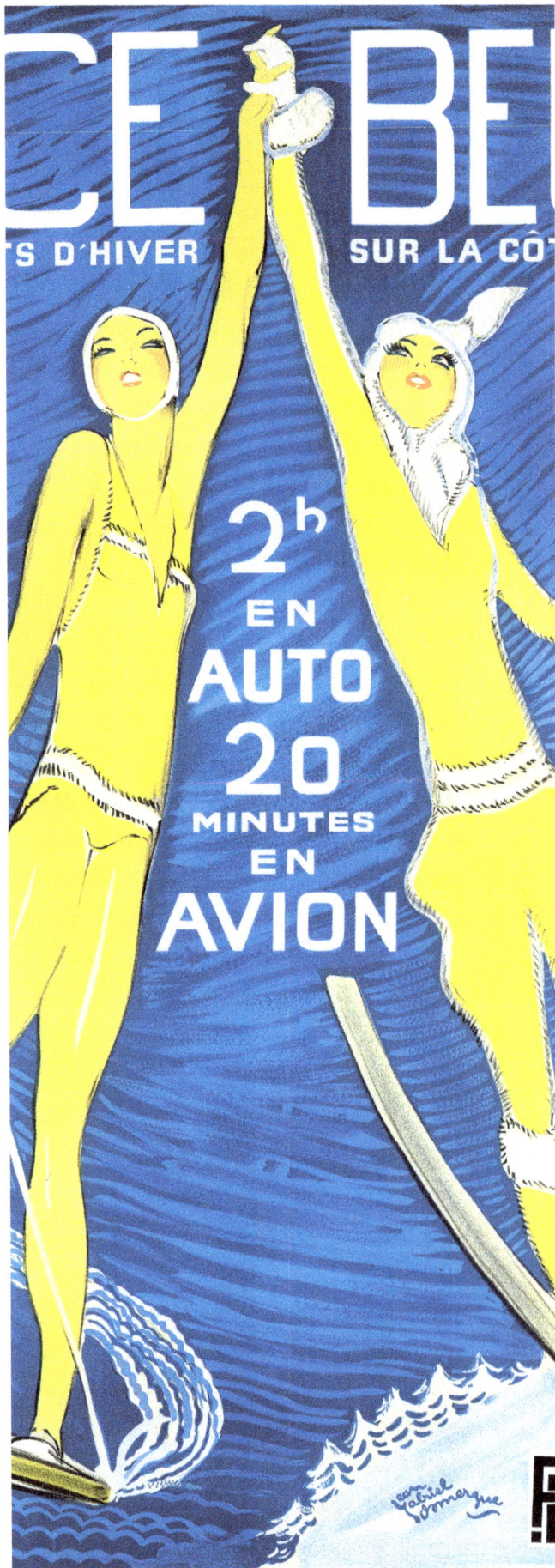

"If you're not losing weight, your exercise isn't working – WRONG."

You need to be fit to attend an aerobics class (now known as group exercise classes) – the class is how you get fit not the other way round. Stand up the back, do what you can, adlib the rest.

If you have a sore knee, treat the knee – nope.

Remember that song "The hip bone is connected to the thigh bone, the thigh bone is connected to the knee bone...?" Well, when one area of the body hurts, it is often also influenced by another area. It's amazing how often my clients with chronic shoulder pain have low back pain as well.

Treating one specific area doesn't address the rest of what is going on in there! Our bodies are very good at compensating and finding the easiest way to do something. If we can't squeeze our shoulders back, we'll arch our lower back by tilting our hips to create a similar movement. This compensatory action can create strain or overuse of the lower back muscles.

If you're not losing weight, your exercise isn't working – WRONG. There are endless benefits to exercise, and I will gladly list a few for you – improved heart health, lung health and mental health, decreased the risk of cardiovascular disease, type 2 diabetes and many cancers. Regular exercise reduces the inflammation in your body, decreasing strain inside and out.

There is more, but I have a word limit, you get the point though.

To find out more about Sarah and her work go to www.wholebodyhealthandwellness.com.au

The Small Town Boy Who Undressed Marilyn

ORRY-KELLY AN AUSSIE IN HOLLYWOOD

by Cassidy Krygger

From a small country town in New South Wales to dressing Hollywood stars such as Marilyn Monroe and designing costumes for some of the biggest movies on the silver screen, Orry-Kelly's rise to success was astounding.

He was once the most famous Australian in Hollywood and was the Aussie with the most Academy Awards to his name until 2014, having won three over his thirty year career. And yet, in his home country, barely anyone knew about him and after his death in 1964, he became virtually forgotten. So who is Orry-Kelly, Australia's first Hollywood legend?

Orry George Kelly was born in 1897 in Kiama, New South Wales and from a young age, had aspirations to be on the stage. To divert him to something more respectable, his mother sent a 17 year old Orry to Sydney to study banking. This wasn't a wise move on Mrs Kelly's part, because his love for the theatre only flourished more in the Harbour City. Orry inserted the hyphen and removed the George and became the glamourous Orry-Kelly when he moved to New York in 1922 to finally pursue a career in acting.

He shared an apartment with a handsome young man who had just arrived from the UK by the name of Archie Leach who also had aspirations to be a star. The pair, according to Kelly, shared an on and off relationship for the next few years until Archie Leach was shipped off to Hollywood to become Cary Grant.

Meanwhile, his acting career wasn't fairing much better. After literally dropping a few chorus girls during a dance number (he admitted to having weak arms), it was decided he was best to do something behind the scenes. Kelly began to work on the costumes and designing stage sets, gaining notice of some Hollywood heavyweights such as Warner Bros. executive Jack Warner.

CONT...

Hollywood beckoned in 1932 and Orry-Kelly found himself moving to the West Coast where he was hired by Warner Bros as a chief costume designer. Orry-Kelly finally hit his stride and he found where he belonged. He designed the costumes for almost 300 films including for iconic movies such as Casablanca, An American in Paris and Some Like it Hot where he designed one of Marilyn Monroe's most iconic and sexy outfits.

He became Bette Davis' most relied upon costume designer early on in her career, she would refuse to do a film if he wasn't designing her costumes. What made Orry-Kelly extraordinary and forward thinking was that while most studios at the time reused costumes to save money, he created costumes for the characters and the actors who were portraying them.

One to never forget his roots, Orry-Kelly visited Australia as often as he could and kept his thick Aussie accent, which must have seemed alien to the Old Hollywood elite. Throughout his time in Hollywood, Orry-Kelly spent his time writing a memoir of his experiences. Something that put Cary Grant on edge, who ended up being able to block the publication in the 1960s.

Orry-Kelly passed away from liver cancer in 1964. Cary Grant was a pallbearer at his funeral. May we never forget him, a boy with a dream who lived life to the absolute Hollywood hilt.

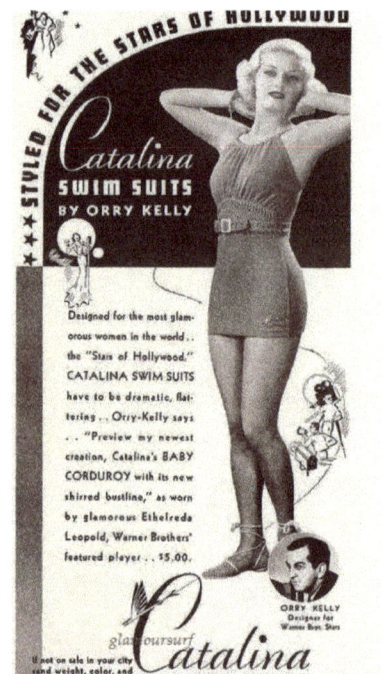

THE FAMOUS MRS FANNY FINCH

BY CASSIDY KRYGGER

On the 18th of August 2020, it was the 100th anniversary of the 19th Amendment in the United States, meaning it was a century ago that some women in the US finally had the right to vote.

The anniversary was widely and justifiably celebrated throughout America and in turn, was all over my social media feeds. And it got me thinking, what about women's suffrage in Australia? Who were the women who fought long and hard so that women could vote?

I was happy to discover that we were almost two decades ahead of our American friends with Australian women over the age of 21 given the right to vote in 1908. Of course, this does not include Victorian Indigenous women who could not vote until 1965.

But there was one woman who cast her vote in Victoria 52 years before women's suffrage was achieved. On January 22nd, 1856 – businesswoman Mrs Fanny Finch cast her vote in Castlemaine, Victoria and wrote her name in the history books.

Fanny was born Frances Combe in London, 1815. An orphan from birth, she believed her parents to be of African descent.

She grew up in the St Pancreas Fledgling Home which protected her from slavery and provided her with an education. In 1836 at the age of 21, she was granted free passage to the new colony of South Australia as a servant of the well regarded surgeon William Wyatt.

Within the decade of arriving in Australia, Fanny had left the employ of Mr Wyatt and his artist wife Julia, and had married a sailor by the name of Joseph Finch.

CONT...

It mustn't have been a joyful union because by 1850 and for reasons unknown, the now Mrs Fanny Finch had left her husband and with her four kids in tow, walked her way from South Australia to Victoria.

Mrs Finch was about to strike gold, arriving in Victoria 12 months before the Gold Rush began. She and her children settled in Castlemaine, which at one point in the 1850s was one of the richest goldfields in the world. 30,000 people descended on Castlemaine from all around the world and Mrs Finch quickly became a successful businesswoman with her very own restaurant and boarding house.

Rumours abounded that her business was a place for the more impolite side of society. A place where a person could get some sly grog and a woman to sleep with for the night. And in 1855 she was persecuted for selling illegal spirits. In an astounding move for a woman at the time, Mrs Finch defended herself and demanded an apology letter from the Mount Alexander Times, which was the newspaper that had reported on her trial.

But it was in 1856 that Fanny Finch etched her name in history when in the Castlemaine elections, she and another anonymous woman cast their votes. And they did it legally. The Municipal Institutions Act of 1854 stated that "any rate-paying persons' which Mrs Finch as a businesswoman was, could vote.

Scandal followed soon after. Melbourne newspaper The Argus reported on the event, called her the 'Famous Mrs. Fanny Finch' and her actions the 'incident of the day'. Election officials disallowed the women their votes on the basis that 'women had no right to vote.' And in 1865 the Municipal Institutions Act of 1854 was amended to exclude women from voting by changing the law from "any rate-paying persons' to "any rate-paying men."

Fanny Finch died in 1863 at the age of 48 and was buried in an unmarked grave. It wasn't until January 2020, that the Victorian Government and Fanny's descendants erected a headstone in her honour at Castlemaine cemetery.

A woman fighting for survival in a male dominated world. A single mother. A woman of colour. And the first woman to vote in Victoria. Why has the famous Mrs Fanny Finch been allowed to fade away to history? And it has got me thinking, what other influential and now unknown people lurk under the dusty pages of our history books?

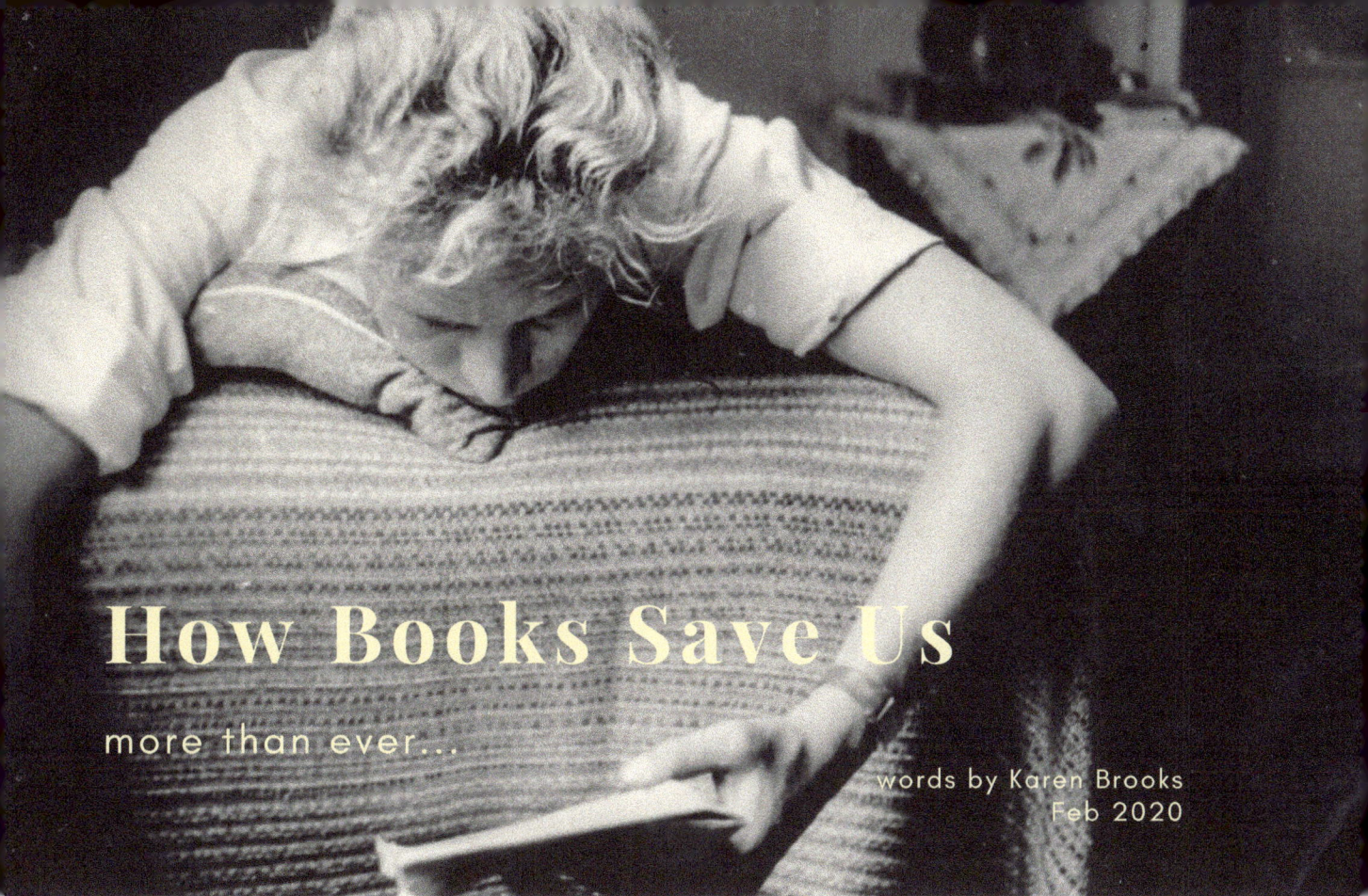

How Books Save Us

more than ever...

words by Karen Brooks
Feb 2020

Here we are at the tail end of a year that, in its numerical configuration alone (2020) promised so much. Instead of clarity, pragmatism and all the other positive meanings that arise when we used to think of 2020, many of us have encountered sickness, death, loss of income, stability, isolation, family crises, never mind sadness, fear, and familial, social and state divisions.

Throughout these long months, the arts - music, dance, poetry, prose, films, TV, clips and events on social media etc - have played an enormous role in helping us cope with the harsh reality of Covid-19 and its fallout - including the endless dismal and doom-laden news-cycle. This has enabled us to appreciate, perhaps in ways we haven't before, the integral role the arts play in helping us understand and define what it is to be human.

"After all, when the going seems tough, there's always a story to fall into, a lexical journey to embark upon, and sometimes quite literally lose yourself in."

Books and fiction especially provide a measure of unquantifiable comfort in harrowing times. They allow readers to escape, even briefly, the cruel or mundane veracity of the everyday and walk vicariously in someone else's shoes, to safely experience their emotions and undergo a journey that, more often than not, resolves in a satisfying way. According to recent studies, reading has increased anywhere from 37% - 41% during the pandemic.

While some folk sought eschatological narratives (end of the world scenarios) in order to perhaps channel their own fears, others turned to the classics, re-read old favourites, reached for their enormous TBR piles – some of which contained books they'd been promising themselves for decades (War and Peace anyone?), found the time to increase their knowledge around certain topics (racism, politics, history etc), or took the opportunity to read genres they've never tried before.

One British study simplified people's choices as those who "read for exploration and those who re-read for safety".

At home, curled up in a chair or in bed, reading of other people, periods and places, is a panacea that both soothes the soul and fires the imagination. It reminds us that while we might be doing it hard (whether that's because of the pandemic, loss, grief, sad memories, poor health, relationship issues, anger, parenthood etc), struggling or triumphing, these are what humans have done since time immemorial. We're remarkably resilient.

Sometimes, the only way to recognise and appreciate that characteristic, to understand we too will get through this, is within fiction.

CONT...

What's evident is that books offer something few other options can: they're the word equivalent of comfort food and we're hungry for it.

Gratitude for what creative artists have given us during lockdown - through their books, art, music, film, dance, TV, social media, cyber-performance etc - has been loud and clear right around the world. What a pity our government cannot acknowledge the importance of the arts and artistes; their intrinsic social, cultural and personal value, choosing instead to cut funding to important bodies and prizes, or offer meagre and competitive grants and loans - and at a time when both the creators and the grateful public need the arts most.

Creative artists are both inventors and curators of culture, of our collective imaginations and hearts. Their work worms its way into our souls and minds, becoming part of individual histories, our memories; they're a short-cut to a moment in time, even to a version of ourselves we no longer recognise - for better and worse.

Books allow us to escape the nightmare of the present (or past) and dream of other spaces, possibilities; of different ways of being. They enable us to move beyond the present and imagine a different future and even, in our darkest moments, a better one.

To read more about the fabulous Karen Brooks head to: https://karenrbrooks.com

COMMUNICATION INSIGHTS AND GETTING GROUNDED IN A WORLD OF CHAOS

BY DES CARTER AND KIRSTEN MACDONALD

Communicating with others can sometimes feel like a minefield. There are so many messages, perceptions and neurone firing, something that should be easy can be anything but simple!

We asked Des Carter; Kinesiologist, Linguistics Practitioner, Holistic Human Development Therapist and Meditation Teacher about his insight into communication.

He shares with us:

Communication is a two-way process of sending and receiving messages and is effective when each person understands each other, however this two-way process can easily break down.

Have you observed the people who only want others to listen to them, but do these people also understand that they need to listen to other people as well? With the principle of listening also comes the ability to effectively understand the things around us.

Clear communication can be blocked when misunderstandings arise due to:

- Different emotional states

- Difference in personal values

- Incongruence between verbal and non-verbal communication

- Difference in the ways people interpret messages

If we listen to what we say and what we think, we would actually understand whether we're making any sense or not. Clarity is not all about the way you manage the outside world, the answer is to go within yourself and manage your inner being that will enable you to identify the lack of clarity.

Remember: whatever requires clarity needs to be understood and if we don't understand something, we need to take time to ask questions and listen to others.

To maintain attention in communication and situations, the "Grounding Technique" is a great way to calm the chatter of your mind. It also improves co-ordination and increases mental clarity and alertness.

Here's how to do it:

Bend your knees a little and position your tongue on the roof of your mouth behind your top teeth, shrug your shoulders and shake your arms for a few moments to free up any tension.

Now focus on your feet and imagine them sinking down into the ground that supports them, imagine them feeling rooted deep into the earth.

Place the fingertips of your left hand beneath your lower lip in the centre of your chin and place the heel of your right hand over your navel with the fingertips of that hand pointing down towards the ground, breathe deeply and gradually slow your breathing down. If you want to, you can imagine the colour red at the base of your spine, deep earthy red. Stay like this and hold your hands on these energy points for the next few moments.

Now push your feet down into the floor and switch hands, breathe deeply and allow yourself to let any tension go from your neck and shoulders. Remain like this for a few moments. Then push your feet down into the floor and switch hands, focus on your feet and imagine them deeply rooted to the earth and remain again for a few moments, breathing deeply and steadily down into your stomach.

Grounding techniques such as this can be a really positive practise in your day to day life. Enjoy! Fo more information about Des go to: https://descarter.com.au

How to Encourage a Love of Reading in Your Children

WRITTEN BY KATIE MOORE

The benefits of reading are hugely impactful in many different areas of your child's life, and not just in the classroom.Reading builds your child's imagination, increases their vocabulary and helps them develop critical social and communication skills that will prepare them well for later in life. Reading can also help kids become more emotionally literate with both 'good' and 'bad' emotions. This, in turn, helps them become more open when it comes to talking about how they're feeling. It's obvious that reading can help your children in school, but studies have shown that it goes beyond mere English lessons.

A UK study by the Institute of Education showed that reading for pleasure can increase a child's cognitive development across many areas, including a 9.9% advantage in mathematics. Reading helps your child build wider knowledge about the world around them, exposing them to different cultures, perspectives and ideas from the comfort of their own home.

This year, and with the onset of the pandemic, our children — and ourselves — are spending more time than ever in front of a screen. Living, learning and evolving online.

Make it a regular activity

Reading regularly with children is very important. The minimum recommendation is to read a book a week with your children. However, I believe that once a day is a better baseline to aim for. Build reading into your child's everyday bedtime routine, and soon it'll become as regular as brushing their teeth.

Select the right book

Having the ability to select the right book seems to be an important factor in children's excitement around reading: nearly three-quarters of kids aged 6-17 (74%) responded to a Scholastic Kids study to say that they would read more if they could find more books that they like.In my own home, I foster my children's love of reading by building excitement throughout the day. Each afternoon we select our bedtime book - one book for each child - and pop it on their beds. My children get so excited to narrow down their book selection that it makes it easier to get them to bed, because they know they have that specially selected book waiting for them.

Give back control

While screen time requires at least some parental control, reading is a safe independent alternative - as long as you've checked the recommended reading age, of course! A trip to the library or bookstore can also help build a sense of ownership around reading, especially if you let the kids have total control over what they select.

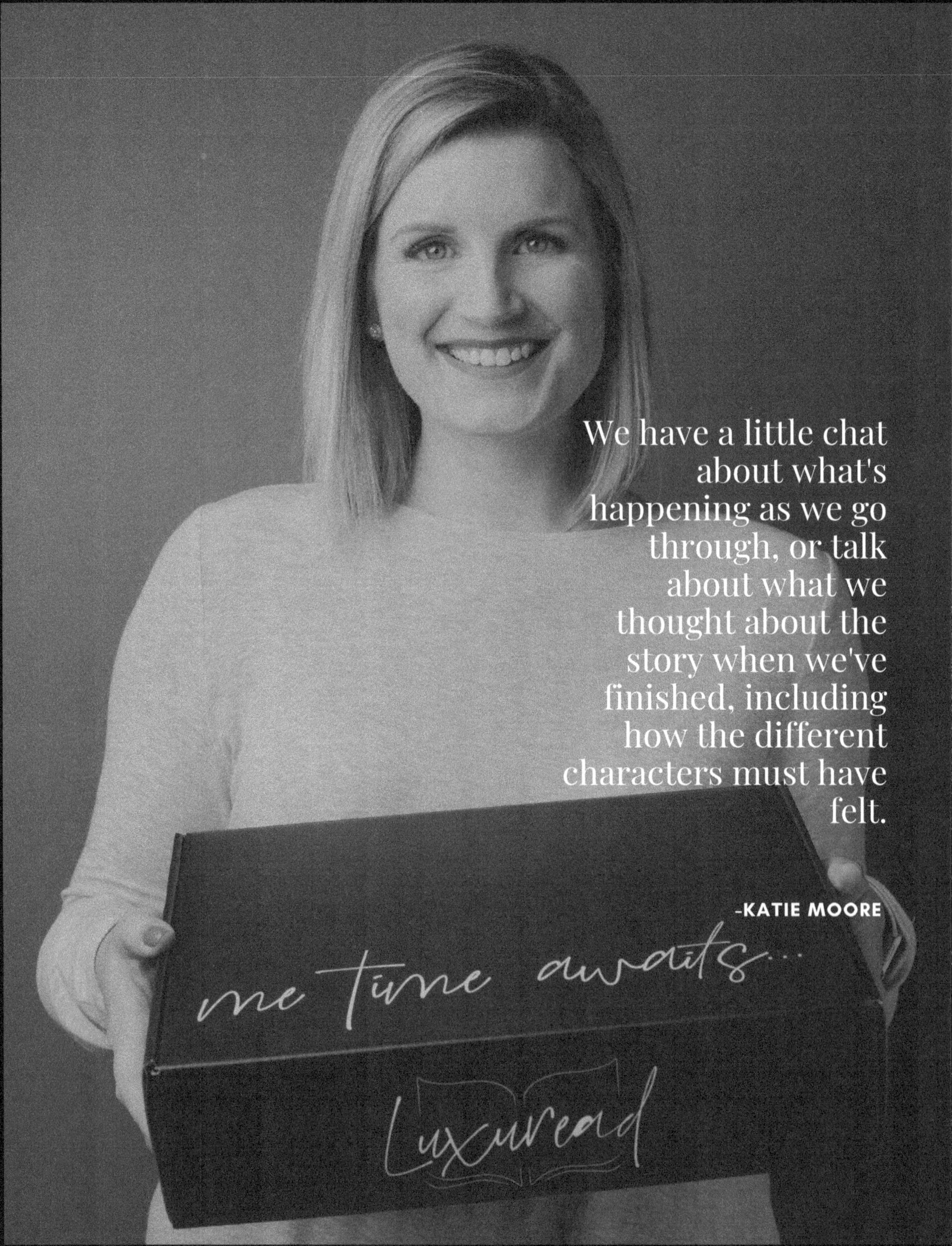

We have a little chat about what's happening as we go through, or talk about what we thought about the story when we've finished, including how the different characters must have felt.

-KATIE MOORE

me time awaits...

Luxuread

CONT...

Start a discussion

Try to build a discussion around the books we're reading, instead of simply shutting the book and being done with it. Instead, we have a little chat about what's happening as we go through, or talk about what we thought about the story when we've finished, including how the different characters must have felt. It's a great way to help their comprehension of the story and work on building their emotional vocabulary.

Start young

While it's never too late to introduce a child to books and reading, it's ideal to nurture it in them from birth. It doesn't always have to be a traditional written story per se: you can still find a lot to explore in a basic picture book, with many different things to point out and talk about through illustration alone.

To find out more about our contributor Katie from Luxuread go to www.luxuread.com.au

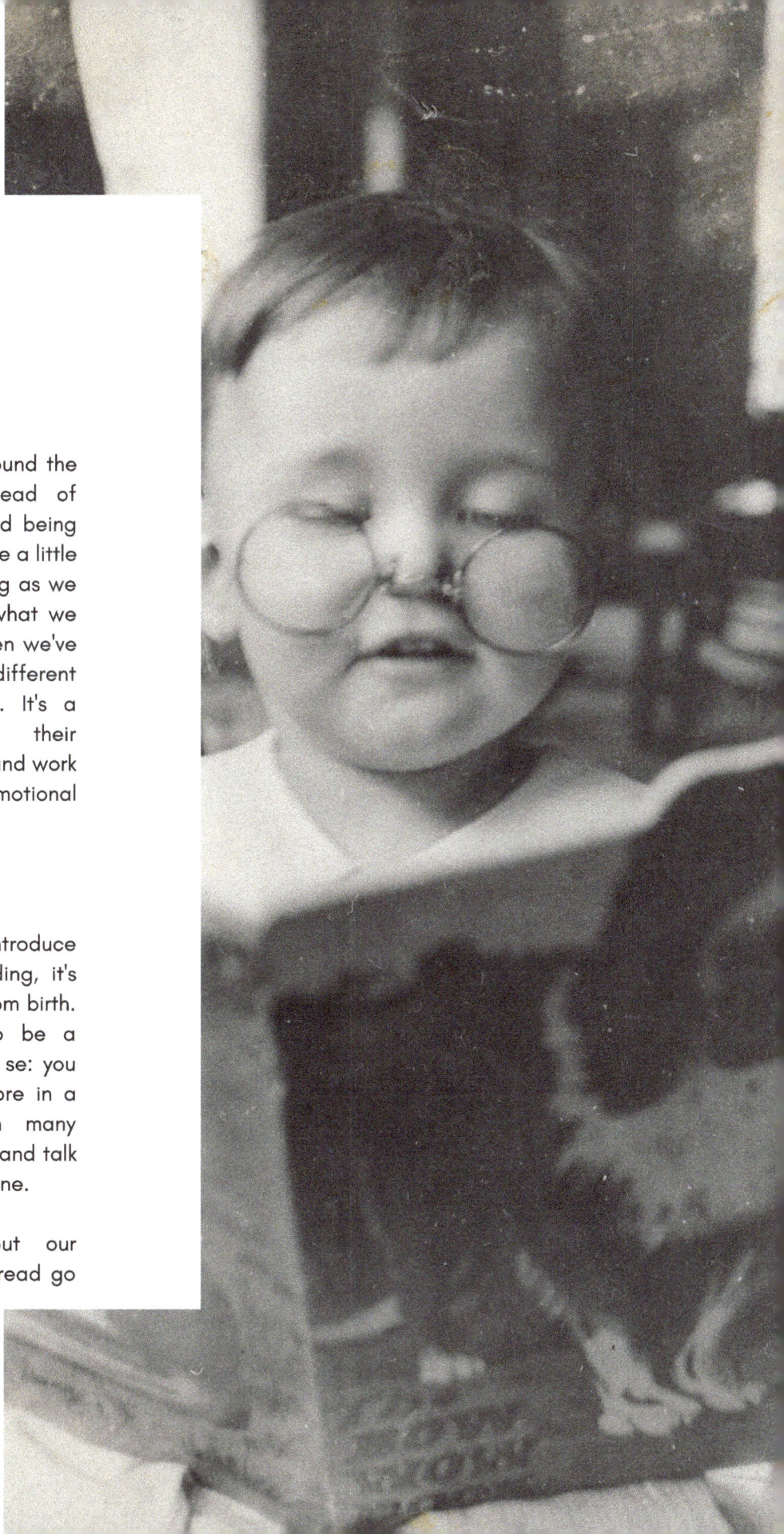

Messages of Hope

From Brisbane-based Poet Tom Stodulka

WORDS BY RENAE FAILLA

*Around the world, lockdown and isolation
continue with long term impacts of COVID-19
lurking, many are struggling to come to terms
with what a COVID Normal will look like.
Tom Stodulka, named 2019 Australasian Mediator
of the Year is reinforcing messages of positivity
in these challenging times.*

Contrasting COVID-19 to experiences of war, he reminds Australians of how we have overcome and survived what has been thrown at us.

"Sometimes it is easy to forget that as a nation, we've survived wars, conflicts, depressions, and economic uncertainty all before COVID-19, and stresses focusing on the small moments of positivity to help get us through...We should remember that life is about enjoying what we can in every single moment. Enjoy the world around you, because happiness is found in every single one of those moments, especially when you're being active and creative."

Tom is no stranger to life's hardships, with his birth taking place in Bathurst 1951 in one of Australia's post-WWII refugee camps after his parents fled Czechoslovakia in 1947 during a time of political unrest, while his older brother was born in a UN Displaced Persons Camp in Italy. His parents primarily spoke German in his childhood years, which added an extra burden to his school years and English essay writing. Seemingly a very distant memory, Tom went on to study law, join the Royal Australian Navy and secure a full-time career as a mediator and facilitator.

He is now an inspiration to people all over Australia. With three reprints of his first book and the support of his loving wife and three children, Tom now hopes to spread messages of hope to Australians experiencing their own hardships.

His new book Life is a Dance, explores the way in which we are challenged as life unfolds, but despite whatever is thrown our way, life is about enjoying what we can in every single moment. Hence, Life is a Dance, not a journey.

Tell us more about your latest book.

It's exciting to have a second book out there called Life is a Dance. It's a follow on from a previous book that I wrote about two years ago called Storm Clouds and Silver Linings: My Journey.

CONT...

I thought rather than repeat the word 'journey' I would try and look at things from a different perspective and again look at things positively with 'Life is a Dance'.

Someone then said to me when they stumble they did part of a dance, and I think that's very positive.

Fun fact: The cover of Life is a Dance features the backdrop of a painting of a Bush Fire scene that Tom's Dad had painted in the 80s. He selected it as the cover of "Life is a Dance" as Australia was going through the intense bushfires last year when the book was being prepared for publication.

Can you tell us what inspires you to write poetry?

It's something that is inspired by nature, our surroundings and people because the poems in both books are about people and about trees and the changes in weather and scenery. Many aspects of nature are a given in our lives, but it's not always positive with storms, cyclones and droughts, but there is always a perception that there is a light at the end of the tunnel.
There's a change in the seasons or a change in the weather.

When you think of the terrible droughts across Australia a year ago and the bushfires and then it's a very Australian thing to think of a return to a better result with sea change in the weather and people have been over the moon across the country to have their dams full again or to be able to grow plants and agriculture is thriving in many ways again thanks to the changes of the weather.

There's a connectivity between everybody and everybody in Australia is affected by the things that occur right across the country.

So many people have been looking for positives despite all the stresses that they have experienced. Just to hear today that all the kids are going back to school today in Victoria and its sort of like a new beginning for so many people - there's an amazing hope again. There are some people who have really struggled with COVID and the lack of connection with their friends and family. As you may know, I am a mediator, so I work a lot with families with conflict and dispute, and that's something that from working in the field you're always looking at remaining positive.

> **"I'M VERY INSPIRED BY PEOPLE, AND WHAT THEY ARE DOING LIKE THE PEOPLE LIVING WITH VERY SERIOUS ILLNESSES. THESE PEOPLE THAT HAVE LIVED THROUGH SOME OF THE MOST TRAGIC EXPERIENCES CAN COME OUT BEING SO POSITIVE."**

During the COVID-19 what has kept you inspired?

Always to think in a positive light because magazines like yours that are real community literature, I've been reading those because magazines like that are able to pick up what's happening in society and what people are doing, what's inspiring people to keep going or do things differently. All these new ideas – fantastic new ideas like Food Services for people working in hospitals, they were really struggling to get their meals and to virtually keep going. These community incentives, community motivation and community-driven to feed thousands of people that are sort of futurists in a way whether its writers or musicians – some of these writers capture the moment noticing all the good things despite the stresses.

I have developed this perspective as a mediator to work with the concept of a 'glass half full' so you can give it your best shot and get the people you are working with to adapt and adopt an idea or concept of looking at things which can be helpful.

Can you pick one of your most memorable poems and explain why?

On page 42 of my latest book Life is a Dance there is one that is dedicated to my writing teacher Linda Henderson. It was her amazing capacity to inspire and encourage people to recognise that they have actually got something to give by their writing.

This poem talks to the influence of people around you which not only focuses on messages of hope like many of my other poems but is a different aspect of positivity.

To learn more about Tom or purchase his new book Life is a Dance for $24.99, head to his website. https://www.tomstodulkaauthor.com

I AM TOO TIRED TO FRIEND

WORDS BY KATE ODONNELL

DEAR FRIEND

I would love to see you, but here's the thing- I'm exhausted. I reminisce about our 20's, the days of grabbing our sunglasses and wallets and following the music, complaining about uni assignments or how insanely busy work was- ha! We thought we were crazy busy back then... HILARIOUS!

Now faced with the grown-up responsibilities of raising a family, paying bills, a mortgage, working and raising little humans and sleep deprivation.

There has been a shift. There are days when simple pleasures of an empty laundry basket, tidy house and wee free bathroom leave me feeling like the high achiever that just won big on the stock exchange- fist-pumping and confidently cheering whoop-whoop! Only to be brought swiftly back to reality when the dog vomits, I've lost the school notice (again) and have forgotten or missed the memo that it is most definitely NOT a cheese day, and for crying out loud why on earth did you cut the sandwich THAT way instead of THAT way... And this, my friend, is the visual definition of parental bliss.

CONT...

In the 2000's Parental burnout became a scientifically researched syndrome all on its own. The family structure has become more diverse, the to-do list has grown, and it appears we are not alone. The number one complaint of parents? Yep. Exhaustion. We laughingly joke about scheduling in coffee catch-ups for September 2024... but at times it really doesn't seem that far off or even that ridiculous! Parenting and my 30's have bought joy, precious memories and the beginnings of a weird chin hair.

It's also brought shrinking of the squad. Our friends are on their own journeys, many live interstates and some abroad. Ideas of raising our children in a commune, attending the same school and getting together for weekly pasta night and community garden remain one-day dreams.

The term "one-man wolf pack" has never felt so relevant. Although to be fair, when the kids are at school, my squad now consists of 2 gorgeous Labradors, a parrot and yappy Jack Russell.

I am still here. I won't be absent forever. This too shall pass... and I will be there, teacup raised and ready to dance, or nap. Coz you know, naps are awesome!
So, Ponderers, why is life so busy that we can't support each other? Why has our parenting become so singular?

Is it because our priorities have changed? Is it because we feel under pressure to be a certain way? Has parenting become a goal to achieve certain milestones with or is it simply because the world has become so hectic?

THE GREAT AUSTRALIAN POTTERY REVIVAL

AN ANCIENT NECESSITY THAT HAS EVOLVED INTO A MASTERCRAFT; THE ART OF POTTERY IS A BEAUTIFUL PROCESS AND HAS RECENTLY ENJOYED A REVIVAL IN POPULARITY. PONDERERS WELCOME TO SOME OF OUR FAVOURITE POTTERS FROM AROUND AUSTRALIA.

BY RENAE FAILLA

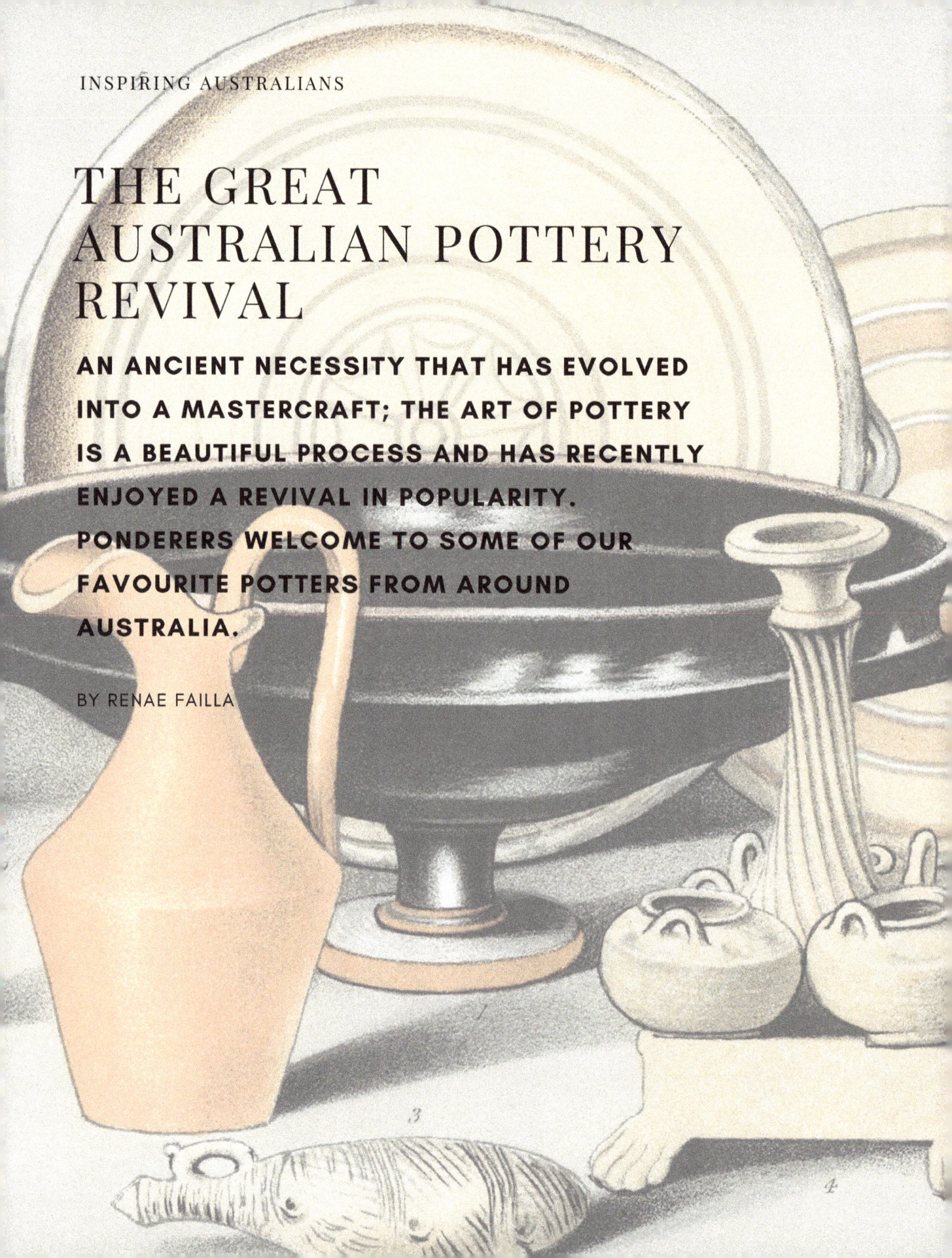

Victoria – Bendigo Pottery

Bendigo Pottery is considered Australia's oldest working pottery, established in 1858 this particular pottery so unique! Why? The pottery still retains a collection of ceramic wood-fired kilns which are some of the only ones left in the world. The kilns are no longer in use but remain in a museum for customers to view. Techniques that are utilised in this pottery are hand throwing, slip casting, jolleying and pressing. You can test out your wheel throwing skills in a half-hour lesson at $18 per person. www.bendigopottery.com.au

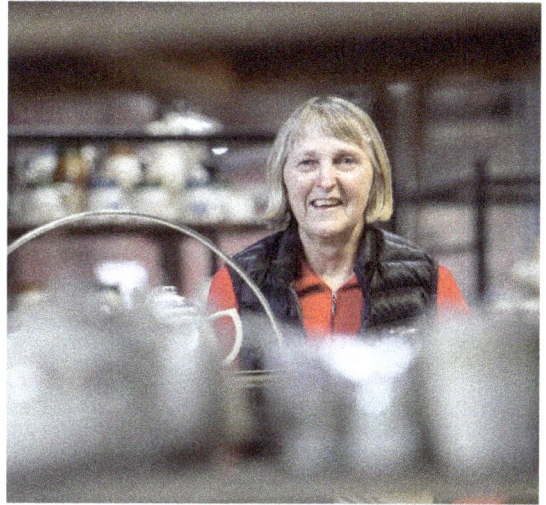

New South Wales – Pilliga Pottery

Pilliga Pottery in New South Wales is family-owned pottery, originating over 30 years ago. Johannes, the son of the original founders, is now the master potter. Utilising local clays, Pilliga Pottery art can be recognised with designs such as the signature Blue Wren and Australian native flowers engraved on their pieces. Their pottery workshops start at $25 per person where you can take home your very own treasure dish.
www.barkalafarmstay.com.au/pottery/pilliga-pottery-studio/

Northern Territory – Tactile Arts

Tactile Arts is a studio that focuses on supporting local emerging artists and creatives through textile and print, ceramics and glass and jewellery classes. Established in 1973, it is considered Darwin's longest-running arts organisation. The organisation holds a yearly schedule of events which includes exhibitions, workshops and a retail store at Parliament House. Workshops here include throwing on the wheel and creating with clay. www.tactilearts.org.au

Tasmania – Small Fires Studio

Small Fires Studio specialises in handmade ceramics for the table, kitchen and Botanics including bowls, espresso cups, mugs, jugs and teapots. Each piece is handcrafted with different washes, glazes and textures and stamped on the bottom with their signature 'Small Fires Studio' mark. Muddle Ceramics Workshops are the linked workshops for the studio, offering adults and kids multiple workshops.. www.smallfiresstudio.com.au

Western Australia – Winterwares

Winterwares derived its name from the creative founder's mother's maiden name 'Winter', her love for the season and the notion that "meals are considered more in winter". Founder Simone Habholz left her fast-paced day job, attempted a pottery class and fell in love with art where she later developed her own range. Winterwares focus on monochromatic designs and employ the Japanese tradition of wabi-sabi to create a luxury range of plates, bowls, mugs and vases. www.winterwares.com.au

South Australia – Studio Potters

With a lengthy history, The 'South Australian Studio Potters Club' as it was formerly known, was established in 1954. Now known as Studio Potters SA, the studio encourages the social and teaching aspect of pottery to help members advance and achieve their goals in all types of pottery. Members pay for their usage of the club, and there is also a sales/exhibition area which faces onto Fourth Avenue. The store exhibits work by the artists from the club including platters, plates, mugs, bowls and pots. Pricing and availability can be found upon enquiry. www.studiopotters.com.au

Queensland – Colour My Pot

This little pottery is a step ahead offering classes guaranteed to spark creativity with pieces ready to be picked, painted, fired, glazed and collected by you. Pieces to paint start at $6 a piece with an additional $10 studio fee otherwise pottery classes are available for $85 per person for a 2.5 hour class. Especially handy during the COVID-19 restrictions are their take-home clay packs which can be purchased in-store for anyone who lives in Cleveland or delivered for an additional $5 within 40km of Cleveland. www.colourmypot.com

THE GHOST LIGHTS

OF

AUSTRALIAN NIGHTS

writen by Montanna Macdonald

Paranormal Investigator Craig Powell recalls the time he witnessed a Min Min light in the dead of night.

"There is the old wives tale, hundreds of years ago, you know you don't follow the Min Min lights, or you will get lost. But you wanted to, everything in your body was telling you to follow it, go towards it, see what it is."

You may have heard of the spooky Australian folklore about the Min Min lights around the campfire, in Aussie shows like McLeods Daughters, Slim Dusty songs, or maybe you have witnessed this hair raising phenomena yourself. With hundreds of sightings around Australia for thousands of years, perhaps these lights are not a myth?

Often reports of Min Min sightings are in outback regions of Australia at night. Witnesses report a silent circular fuzzy light, quarter the size of a full moon that dances in the dark sky. They claim these balls of glowing light can appear in colours of white, yellow, red, green and even blue, with an edge that looks like a swarm of insects.

CONT...

The erratic nature of a Min Min light is what often frightens those who spot one. Known to suddenly divide into two lights and appear like headlights in the distance, then frantically looking to move closer, further, up down and around the horizon. Some claim that Min Min lights have followed their movements as they drive, then disappear. And, as the old folktale goes, those who follow the Min Min light often never return.

This mystery has been around for thousands of years, Australia's First Nations people say these lights have appeared more frequently since settlement.

It is unclear when sightings began, and due to the oral traditions of these indigenous stories pre-settlement, there is not a substantial amount of written evidence of sightings and indigenous names for these lights.

Aboriginal studies researchers such as Larrakia man and Senior Lecturer at Charles Darwin University, Dr Roman, have found consistencies in light descriptions among Indigenous communities. For example, the lights being like snakes, which could be connected to the Indigenous belief of the rainbow serpent, and that they have a 'guardian role' on sacred sites.

The name Min Min was adopted in 1918, named after the small Min Min settlement and Hotel in between the two Northern Queensland towns Boulia and Winton. The story goes that a stockman was riding his horse down the Kennedy development road past the now burnt down Min Min Hotel when suddenly a light appeared above the graveyard that was behind the premises. Boulia is now a major tourist hotspot for Min Min sightings. These lights are not just in Boulia; there are sightings predominantly on fine winter nights among the Channel Country of South Australia, New South Wales, Queensland, Northern Territory and in the Kimberleys in Western Australia.

The lights have been spotted all year round, including above seashores. Not only in Australia, but similar mysterious lights have been seen in Saudi Arabia, called Abu fanoos. Similarly, global folklore lights exist, such as ghost lights, ignis fatuus, the Celtic will o' the-wisp, Mexico's brujas, South America's luz mala, phantom lights and fairy lights.

Paranormal Investigator Craig Powell shared with Ponderings his own Min Min light experience when on a field research trip in the notorious NSW Pilliga Forest. This is what Craig had to say:

"This light appeared, but the light started pulsating, and it would get really bright, and it got really dim, and then it would start dancing around through the bush. At one stage the one light broke into two lights. They would change colours from like a bright white to an orange type colour. It would look like it would come down the gorge towards us, and then it would look like it was heading back away from us. So we sat there, and we watched these two lights dancing around the forest. It was one of the most amazing things I've seen.

If we go out on a night hike, we travel that route during the daytime hours, so we get our bearings, and know exactly what points we want to stop. You take yourself back to the daytime where we were sitting, and you think well what's down there? And it was like a big cliff so these lights would've been coming up halfway up on a cliff. You think about it; there is no way a possible person could get to that position, especially at night time, it was really odd. The light seemed to disappear at one point, and then we just continued on our way back to camp."

Now it wouldn't be a mystery without a few hypotheses. What is a Min Min light? Can it be debunked with a scientific explanation, or is this phenomenon a conspiracy of the unexplainable? In different First Nations legends, the Min Min lights are elders protecting the country. First Nations people in the Channel Country don't regard the Min Min lights positively, but also not harmfully. Conspiracy theories for the Min Min lights also include you guessed it...aliens, UFOs and ghosts. However, polymath and neuroscientist Professor John Pettigrew has several hypotheses.

Bioluminescence from birds, insects and fungi is a possible theory. Still, no one has ever caught or observed these proposed organisms maintaining the intense illumination and circular shape of a Min Min light. Another is burning marsh gas, which is a well-known phenomenon causing what is called the will o' wisp, but this natural occurrence lacks the shape, height and brilliance of Min Mins.

The most probable theory is the Min Min lights is a refraction phenomenon, otherwise called an inverted Fata Morgana; a mirage. A Fata Morgana is where light in the day can be reflected from a hot ground layer of air, like when you see the sky reflecting on a hot road when driving.

CONT...

Similarly, an inverted Fata Morgana mirage occurs at night, a temperature inversion can occur, where a cold ground layer of air can refract light due to a gradient increase in refractive index, meaning the light can appear above the horizon.

It can travel over the horizon for hundreds of kilometres with possible magnification, reduced dispersion and dissipation. Natural atmospheric light and human-made lights like headlights can cause phenomena.

Pettigrew in 1992 made his own Min Min light. On a cold calm night, he drove his car 10km North of his camp where it is not viewable from the campsite. As the headlights were on, campsite observers confirmed via radio the headlights were causing phenomena with the characteristics of a Min Min light. When the headlights were off, the light also vanished. A Fata Morgana mirage is also common overseas, where sea cliffs in Ireland can be seen clearly in the middle of the North Atlantic sea, even though they are hundreds of kilometres away from their location.

Documentary filmmaker Don Meers created the critically acclaimed AustrAlien Skies series, with the third 2019 film dedicated to the "Search For The Min Min." This documentary is a must-watch, exploring the varying theories with balanced scepticism and in-depth research. Don also appears to catch the Min Min phenomena on camera.

When Ponderings asked Don about how it felt to finally catch a Min Min light, he said:

"We were on location for many days, staying up through the night, camera-ready, resting and filming through the day. So you can imagine it was quite exhausting. By the time we actually saw the light, it was like a rocket taking off. It's an instant hit of adrenaline after many nights of nothing. Your brain just goes into overdrive."

CONT...

Don believes the majority of sightings are explainable, being misidentified causes like distant headlights or mirages. Still, he also explains:

"Temperature inversions need specific climate conditions to manifest. One main factor is that they can usually only happen in winter and surrounding cooler months, and because of climate change, scientists are noticing a significant drop-off. So I think that they can explain a lot but not all and that more research is needed. I think there are a lot of plausible explanations for Min Min lights, but there is still an outlying percentage that is unexplained as yet."

You can watch the series across the major streaming platforms including iTunes, Google, Amazon Prime, Hulu and more. The Min Min lights remain one of Australia's biggest mysteries, and whether you are the sceptic, the witness, or the mystically minded, remember, if you ever find yourself in the Australian wilderness in the dark, you won't find the lights, they find you.

OLYMPIC SPORT; THE BIRDS EYE VIEW OF ART

WRITTEN BY MONTANNA MACDONALD
PHOTOS BY BRAD WALLS

Have you ever wondered what sports look like from a bird's eye view? Well, this is what Sydney Based photographer Brad Walls set out to explore.

Brad Walls, known as Bradscanvas, is an aerial photographer. Keeping it unique with drone photography, Brad adds flair to scenes such as sport; showing the art form of us. Winning the Skypixel awards for his synchronised swimming team photo series this year, Brad explores a different perspective of Olympic sports like tennis, ice skating, gymnastics and synchronised swimming.

Brad photographs the world from the eye of the sky that genuinely leaves you in awe; imagery using symmetry and majestic patterns creating art with geometric flair.

We pondered, how does Brad get these fantastic shots from above so perfectly?

Where did your photography journey start? What do you love about the art form?

As a teenager, I was quite creative, borrowing friends' cameras, playing with 3D software, building stuff with my hands and generally being a curious kid. It wasn't until I bought a drone that I began to take it seriously. I started with video snippets of clips for Instagram, but it was a lot of work and didn't enjoy the process as much as working on one photographic composition.

I'm drawn to photography as it has the ability to blend creative concepts and the real world, creating a hybrid environment to let your mind wander but also being quite grounded truly.

Can you share with our Ponderers some of your favourite photo series from your works and the meaning behind them, we see you have just released a new series called "Pools From Above"

Great question and obviously a very hard one to answer as each series has their own identity. However, the Pools From Above series are my favourite.

The Pools From Above series sparked a transition in my aesthetic and deep understanding of composition. I remember spending hours trying to perfect this image named "A Palm Springs Ting" on my Instagram. It must have taken me 50 edits to get that image to sing, but that learning process was the foundation of the entire series. I cannot stress the importance of failing time after time to find a winning formula.

What led you to do aerial photography, sport and Olympic photography?

Aerial photography provided a realm of new opportunity within the photography space. A space, which I believe has lacked creative innovation.

The sports series was inspired by the shapes from above. When thinking and exploring, many sports provided those shapes that without an aerial perspective may have never been exposed. As you can see from the synchronised swimming, ice skaters and gymnasts series, all of which offered new and intriguing perspectives.

What is your creative process in deciding what you will photograph and how?

My creative process is varied; it could come from out in the everyday world and spotting a moment or a structure and wondering what that could look like from above. Or it may be looking on Google earth and spotting something that may look beautiful from the air; this method worked particularly well with my 'Pools From Above'.

Ultimately, it comes down to curiosity, as an artist, you constantly need to be curious, questioning "what could be?"

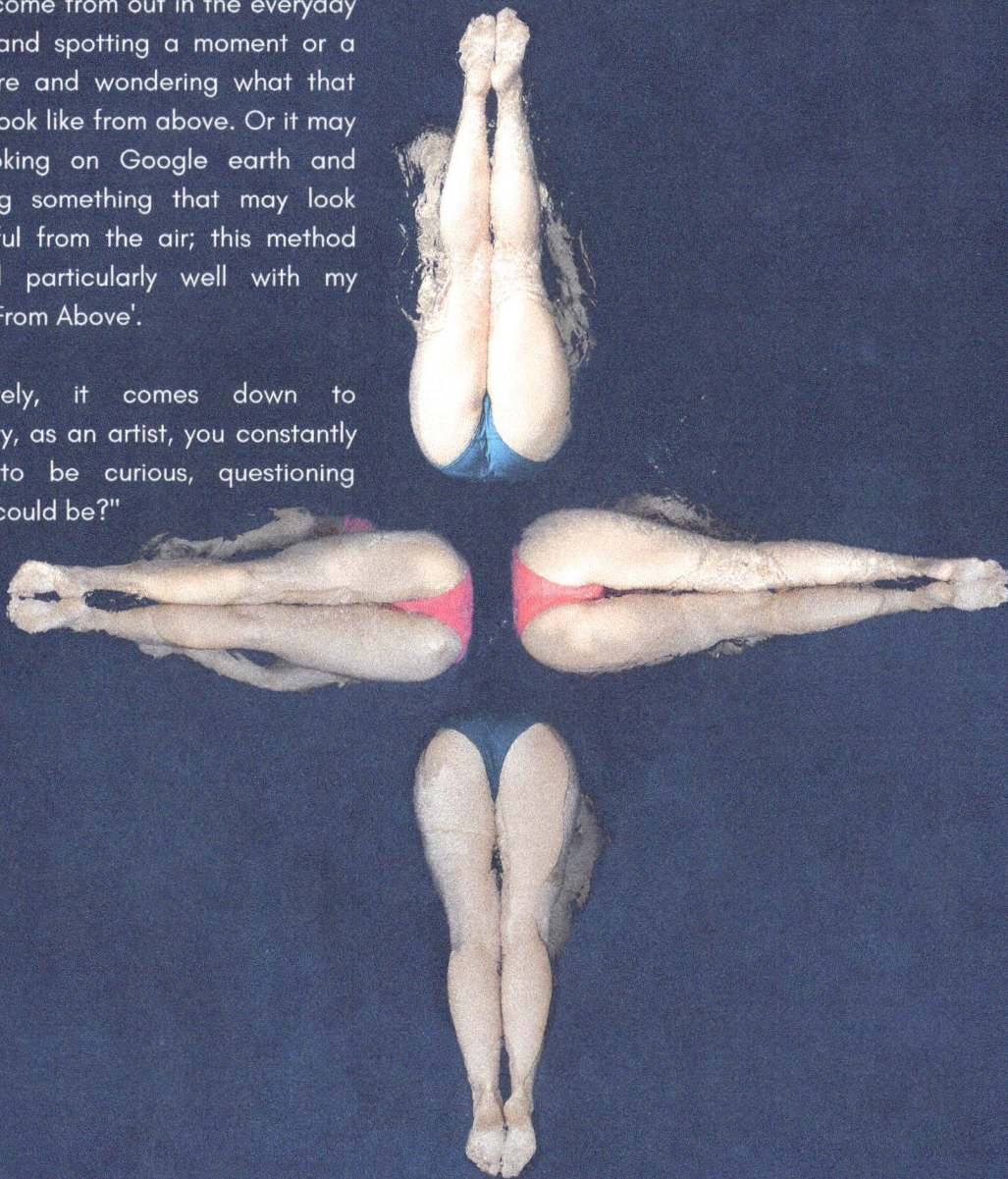

CONT...

Do you have any new series in the works?

I am continually working on my "Pools From Above" series, working towards a coffee table book in the near future. I'm in the middle of launching a series with an Australian Ballerina, which has been very popular with viewers. Watch out on my Instagram for that to drop.

Could you please share with us one of your favourite photo series concepts you have done, and why it is a favourite?

That concept would be the upcoming release with the Australian Ballerina. It's my favourite because I loved the experience of being pushed to try a perspective that hadn't been attempted before, and ultimately that is what drives me to do what I do.

Brad's upcoming Australian Ballerina series is a beautiful perspective that we know you ponderers will appreciate, as well as the many other creative shots Brad captures. You can check out his Instagram @bradscanvas.

FOUR PAWS SAVE BEAR CUBS NIKKO AND NARA

BY MONTANNA MACDONALD

Asiatic black bear cubs' Nikko and Nara have been saved by organisation FOUR PAWS; a bear rescue mission in Vietnam. Ponderings investigates...

FOUR PAWS is a global animal welfare organisation supporting animals, creatures who are victims of human battery in varied and horrific ways. The organisation is a noble one, and their work includes projects in emergency rescue and ongoing care for a great range of different animals.

This year, FOUR PAWS Vietnam rapid response team saved two bear cubs from smugglers from the illegal wildlife trade. The legal and illegal wildlife trade in Vietnam is a billion-dollar industry. Bile farming is the process of breeding bears in captivity. The terrible conditions are made even more atrocious by the shocking bile extraction process from the bear's gallbladder while alive; only to be sold in markets, restaurants, online and used in pseudo-traditional medicines.

CONT...

On the 21st of July, FOUR PAWS were notified of two Asiatic black bear cubs that had been confiscated by the environmental police from wildlife smugglers who were trying to sell the cubs online via social media.

On the 22nd of July, the small FOUR PAWS team made an 11-hour journey to Lai Chau Province at the Vietnam border where they rescued the cubs and brought them to their new home, Bear Sanctuary Ninh Binh.

"Both cubs were very stressed and huffed at anyone trying to approach them. The male is quite protective of the very timid female, hiding in a corner and nestling under him. They will now receive all the care they need to calm down and recover from a turbulent start of their lives. Both cubs are in stable condition, but slightly underweight. Our vets are examining them thoroughly, and once we are sure they are disease-free we will socialise them with another bear cub we rescued earlier this year from similar circumstances," says Emily Lloyd, Animal Manager at Bear Sanctuary Ninh Binh.

The Vietnamese Government announced on the 24th of July 2020, the banning of imports and trade of wild animals.

CONT...

While this is promising after years of effort from FOUR PAWS and fellow animal welfare NGOs, the organisation hopes the Government's efforts to enforce the ban will be effective. Still today, there are over 400 farmed bile bears in Vietnam.

"Although the sale and possession of bear bile are illegal in Vietnam, it still exists as due to weak enforcement of the laws. We hope that this new directive and subsequent revised enforcement efforts will also affect bear farming and eradicate the illegal sale and possession of bile products," says Kieran Harkin, responsible for Wild Animals in Trade at FOUR PAWS.

The Bear Sanctuary Ninh Binh where Nikko and Nara now live is a wildlife conservation education centre and a beautiful, safe home for these furry friends while they heal and grow. Nikko and Nara have made a fellow friend, bear cub Mochi.

The sanctuary, which began construction in 2016, now has six outdoor enclosures, three bear houses, a quarantine station and veterinary unit, a feeding kitchen and an admin building. It can house up to 50 bears now, but once fully finished with construction will be able to provide a species-appropriate home for up to 100 rescued bears.

Currently, all 33 Asiatic bears in Bear Sanctuary Ninh Binh were victims of bile farming and illegal trade. "Our bears often arrive with a multitude of health issues; some are obese, some emaciated, some are even missing paws or limbs from being trapped in the wild. Dental disease is common along with mobility issues and gallbladder and liver infections from the unsanitary bile extraction process.

It is admirable the work FOUR PAWS do to give these bears hope for a better life and future. We asked FOUR PAWS spokesperson Elise Burgess, what does a day in the life of the Bear Sanctuary Ninh Binh look like?

For FOUR PAWS, they do a variety of tasks, from essential rehabilitation and quarantine processes for bears newly rescued, to feeding, medication, general enclosure maintenance but also what they call "environmental enrichment".

CONT...

"An essential part of animal care is 'environmental enrichment', which is necessary for the optimal physical and psychological wellbeing of our rescued bears. The five main categories of enrichment are sensory, cognitive, social, physical habitat and food.

Our outdoor enclosures provide a complex environment where the bears can forage for food, dig, climb, swim, play, hide and rest, all things they would naturally do. In the wild bears spend the majority of the time they are awake looking for food. By presenting our bears' food in different ways such as scattering and hiding it throughout their enclosures, or using puzzle feeder toys, for example, we are allowing our bears to express this natural behaviour.

Bears are thought to have the best sense of smell of all animals on earth, 2100 times better than humans! Therefore olfactory (scent) enrichment is particularly stimulating for bears, so on certain days our bear caretakers put out different scents such as cinnamon, or peppermint, for the bears to investigate."

Now, Ponderers, we hope envisioning bear cubs safe in a beautiful haven sniffing for cinnamon and peppermint brings you all the heart smiles for your day. You can donate to FOUR PAWS at their website, and follow them on Instagram, Facebook and Twitter for updates on the incredible work they do with not only bears but other projects around the world. If you would like to know more information about the Bear Sanctuary Ninh Binh, follow them on Facebook, and when international travel is allowed again, go visit Ninh Binh! You can see the bears in their tranquil haven, purchase locally made souvenirs and enjoy some traditional vegetarian and vegan Vietnamese dishes at the onsite restaurant.
https://www.four-paws.org.au

Five Ways to Identify if Your Workplace is Toxic and What to Do About it

words by Melissa Griffiths

Could you imagine going to a workplace that wasn't toxic? Yes, they do exist.

According to The Barometer Project findings show that depression costs Australian employers approximately AUD $8 billion per annum as a result of sickness absence and presenteeism and AUD $693 million per annum of this is due to job strain and bullying. A prominent finding is that the cost is mostly due to workers showing mild symptoms of depression as they take twice as many sick days as those who do not show any symptoms of depression at all.

CONT...

The results further suggest that potentially AUD $17.84 billion in costs to the employer could be saved if the mental wellbeing of the 25 per cent least psychologically healthy working Australians could be raised to the level of the 25 per cent most psychologically healthy workers.

So what are some of the factors contributing? Let's take a look at some signs in what is a very serious problem for Australians.

Here are five signs that you might be in a toxic workplace, plus some short and long term solutions.

1. Hierarchy

Believe it or not, modern workplaces were constructed after the Industrial Revolution, designed mainly by men. They were built like pyramids, with a clear leader at the top and many minions at the bottom. Obvious power imbalances lead to power games, which occur at the expense of people within the organisation.

2. Futility

Toxic workplaces are NOT productive. When employees are unproductive, they feel any attempt at work is futile. Then they start to focus on other things, including gossip. In the lunchroom about their new colleague whose hair is purple. Naturally, if this person overhears the gossip, they will feel excluded. Which leads to my next point…

ius TOXICODÉNDRON, Linn.

3.Circularity

When people feel excluded, they become even more unproductive. I mean, who wants to work in this kind of environment...? They end up doing the bare minimum, taking sick leave, and withdrawing from their colleagues. If this dysfunction in the workplace is ignored – or even tolerated – by management, it becomes a vicious circle.

4. Expectations

When managers are under heightened pressure, expectations change. Jobs are lost, hours are cut, and sometimes unrealistic expectations are placed on staff. Often, workers are pushed to 'go the extra mile', and personal circumstances – particularly for those in marginalised communities – are not taken into account.

5. Bullying

The clearest sign of a toxic workplace is serial bullying and harassment by those in positions of power. The culture certainly comes from the top. If HR is covering up this behaviour, it simply flourishes.

So, what are the solutions? Well, there are some measures which can be taken to mitigate this, such as ensuring there is proper education about different people's behaviour patterns, effective communication, understanding mental health issues, diversity and inclusion, and leadership skills. Also, you need the right people in the right positions if you have a hierarchical structure. There needs to be an environment of openness and trust, where people know that their concerns are heard and acted upon instead of being ignored. You can do this by going through either internal Human Resources or contacting an external consultant to facilitate training. Building an environment where people are valued creates positive change for all. Where you need consulting or training about constructing a positive work environment – including around diversity and inclusion – reach out to me and let's see how we can work together.

Melissa Griffiths is a transgender authority and workplace advocate. Melissa is also a highly sought after speaker for events and conferences. Check out her details at https://www.melissagriffiths.com.au

Ten Insights into the Narcissist

We hear the word Narcissism in reference to traits of self-interest and vanity in a world of social media. However, Narcissism or Narcissistic Personality Disorder -NPD is a mental condition. A well-balanced perspective is needed along with some tips for those on the other unpleasant end of Narcissistic behaviour.

The excessive need for admiration, disregard for others' feelings, the inability to handle any criticism and a sense of entitlement along with criticism and manipulation, grandstanding (the list goes on) are all facets of Narcissism. Researchers have reported associations between NPD and high rates of substance abuse, mood, and anxiety disorders. For more symptoms see the bottom of this article, we have some excellent references.

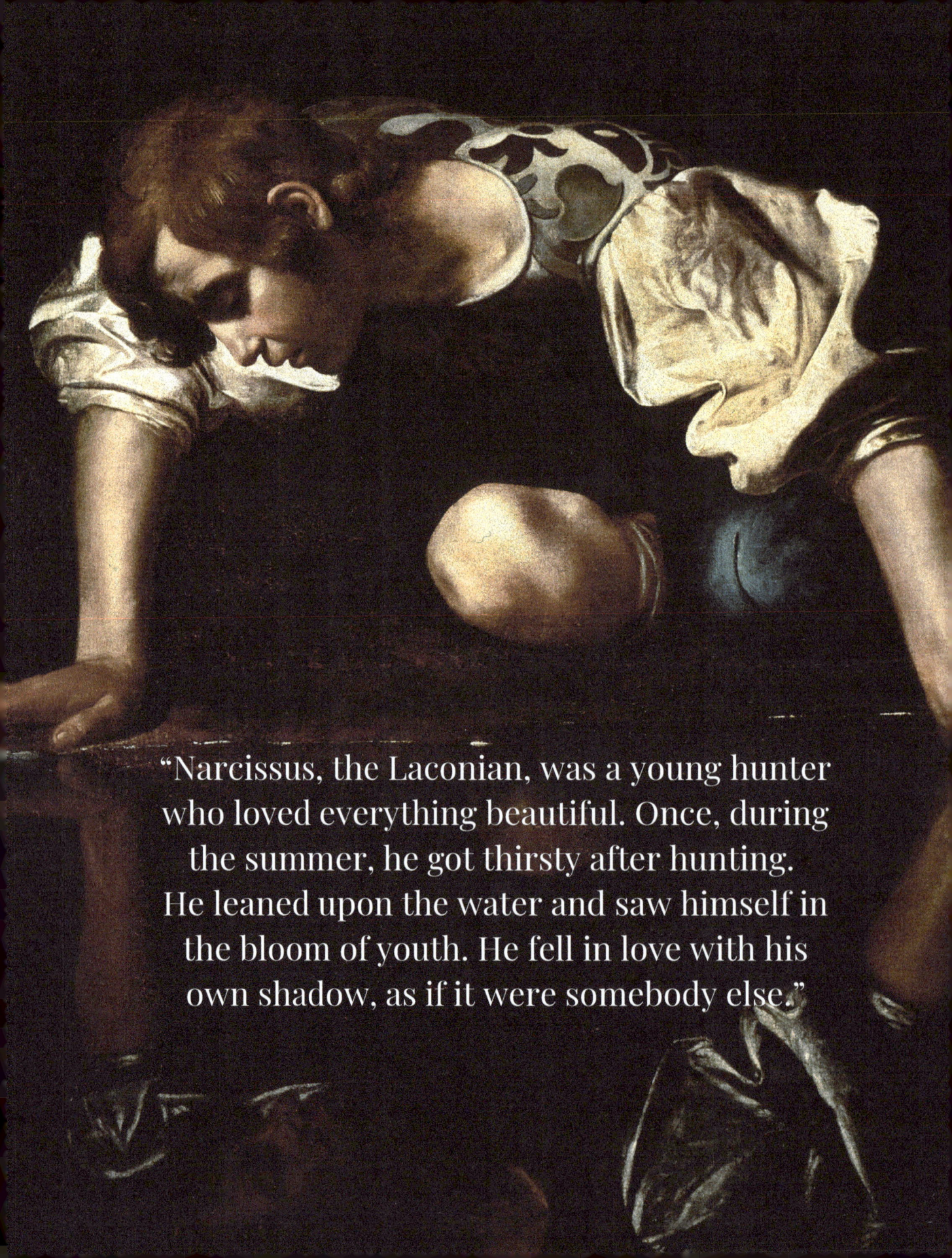

"Narcissus, the Laconian, was a young hunter who loved everything beautiful. Once, during the summer, he got thirsty after hunting. He leaned upon the water and saw himself in the bloom of youth. He fell in love with his own shadow, as if it were somebody else."

Being in a relationship or friendship with a true Narcissist can find you drawing in toxic sludge. Many an injured heart, broken life and mental anguish can be the product of such behaviour. So what can be done?

1) Never admit vulnerability to a Narcissist.
It can and will get used against you in a typical 123 Gaslighting maneuver. Do not appear fragile to a Narcissist, you are a duck on a lake, graceful, your legs might be going nuts underneath, but all anyone can see is serenity. Vulnerability is important with the right person. A Narcissist is not that person.

2) Understand Gaslighting behaviour.
A type of psychological manipulation whereby a person covertly sows seeds of doubt in a targeted individual or group, making them question their memory, perception, or judgment, often evoking in them cognitive dissonance and other changes including low self-esteem.

3) While many people tell you a Narcissistic person is self-centred, mean and arrogant, it is MUCH more complex.
Manifesting in many ways, including an overdeveloped sense of entitlement, a lack of empathy, and a need for admiration, grandiose behaviours, sensitivity to criticism, the list goes on. The point here is- the condition is layered and varied, so unless you are a trained psychologist or therapist; seek professional assistance if you believe you are on the receiving end. It is very dangerous for your mental health and not always obvious. Gaslighting, in particular, can be very insidious.

4) Understanding that while the condition remains somewhat of a mystery to psychology experts; behavioural disorders are often deeply rooted.
You cannot talk a Narcissistic out of anything. Some studies suggest many Narcissists know precisely what they are doing, they believe they are on a higher pecking order than others, view themselves as more evolved, and they are never 'wrong." There is no reasoning here. Try and reason, and you mayl soon find yourself attacked verbally and wounded.

5) If stuck in a verbal corner, try using non-critical words and don't attack or question their motives.

There is no win here. Use phrases with sincerity. Phrases such as "I'm trying to understand what you are saying, leave it with me and I'll come back to you on that one" can help disentangle. You have the option to smile sweetly and say "Well, I'll take that into consideration. I am sorry you feel that way." Make your polite exit. Walk away and keep the tone light.

6) You can have objective empathy, so you can spend less time with the person and try to remember it's okay to do this.

Just because you live near a poisoned lake, doesn't mean you have to drink from it every day and it can still have lovely elements on sunrise. Focus on the positive, but remember it's okay to say no.

7) Do not believe the love bombing.

The Narcissist enjoys making you feel loved up and joyful; this may come in the form of gifts or favours. This makes you fodder; it makes you open up and become vulnerable for an unfortunate future personal attack. Be pleasant, but don't soak it up or take it as gospel. Be objective and don't get attached to incoming feels. They become weapons later.

8) Do not encourage codependency.

Be warned! You need you. Be self-sufficient and do not rely on the person. Relying on people who care about you for support sometimes is okay, this is the essence of community, looking out for each other. But do NOT do this with a Narcissist. This will foster a sense of dependency, so when you do wake up and realise what is happening, you will have emotions, not unlike an addiction.

9) Pay attention!

Long term exposure to Narcissism can make you immune to the behaviour. Keep a note of when you feel awful or manipulated and when you don't. Are you okay at work and with other relationships? Do you have strong bonds with others and feel good? If you only feel poorly around one person, this is a sign of a deeper issue. Ongoing mental manipulation is damaging and will have consequences.

10) Get educated.

You have power in your life to make choices, so you can make them! Perhaps you might like to reclaim your personal power and find out more about these aspects showing up in your life. Why are you making room for them? Do you have to? What will happen if you don't make any changes with this relationship or within yourself concerning this person? What might happen if you do?

Seek help professionally and use the situation to learn about the events in your life.

According to Erika Carlson and co in extensive research; the Narcissist is often fully aware of their reputation and simply do not care. They believe they are genuinely the right one, the most important. Consider for a moment that narcissistic people do not really lack empathy, but instead, their vulnerability and need for self-protection limits their freedom to express it.

Exploiting and bullying others while being the best on show is a standout feature of NPD, and some very strong tricks are used to keep everyone playing out the illusion. So the warning here is if you listen for long enough, even the strongest of minds can and do break under pressure. Calling a person with NPD out can inflame the situation making life much harder for you. Stay calm, collected and reduce your exposure.

**Always seek medical assistance and professional psychological help. Helping yourself is the first step to a positive life. This article is not intended for advice of any professional nature and is an aristic exploration of the topic.

Journals and websites for further reading:

Diagnostic and Statistical Manual of Mental Disorders, Fifth Edition Kacel, E. L., Ennis, N., & Pereira, D. B. (2017).

Narcissistic Personality Disorder Clinical Health Psychology Practice: Case Studies of Comorbid Psychological Distress and Life-Limiting Illness. Behavioural Medicine, 43(3), 156-164Carlson, E. N., Wright, A. & Iman, H. (2017).

Blissfully blind or painfully aware? Exploring the beliefs people with interpersonal problems have about their reputation. Journal of Personality, 85, 757-768. 10.1111/jopy.12284

Getting to Know a Narcissist Inside and OutErika N. Carlson Laura P. Naumann Simine VazireBook Editor(s): W. Keith Campbell Joshua D. MillerFirst published: 20 July 2011https://doi.org/10.1002/9781118093108.ch25Citations:

https://www.skiplab.org/erikahttps://www.helpguide.org/articles/mental-disorders/narcissistic-personality-disorder.htm

https://psychcentral.com/disorders/narcissistic-personality-disorder/https://pro.psychcentral.com/freud-and-the-nature-of-narcissism/

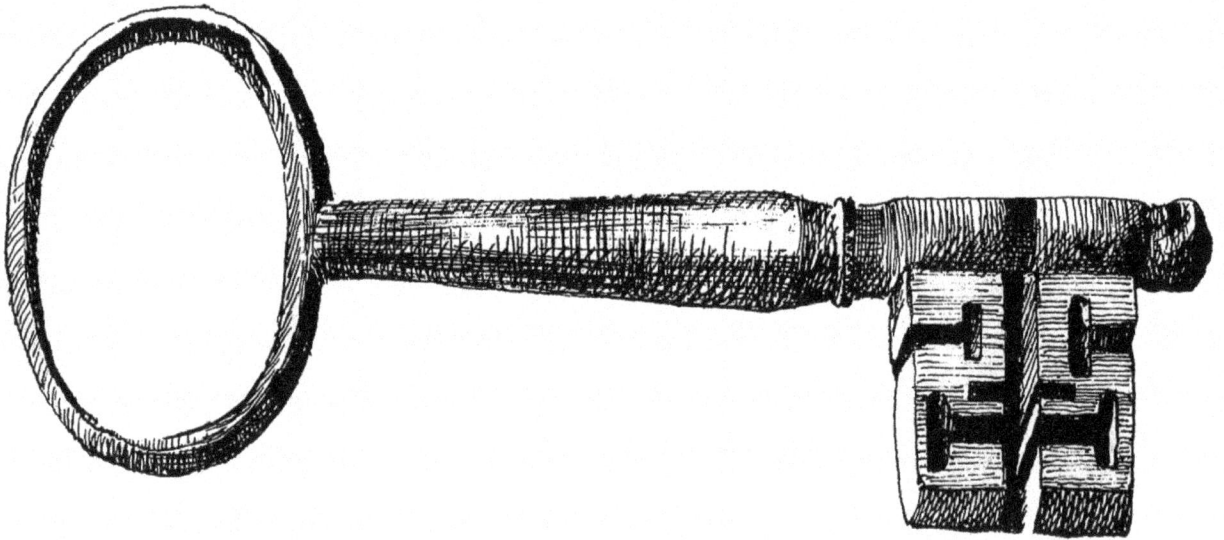

Secret Messages – What You See Is Not What You Always Get

by Kirsten Macdonald

Let me paint you a picture. Two people are in a combative stance. You are all at a BBQ (no more than 10 of course) and these two are clearly unhappy, but there is no yelling. You can see something is up.

How so?

It has to do with all of the information you may be getting about the scene. So what are you picking up on? Most likely, you are witnessing and making discerning decisions about their body language along with the tone they are using and any preconceived knowledge you have of them.

On closer inspection as you move closer to the chips and french onion dip you notice they are indeed having a bit of a verbal stoush.

One person's words you note are not overtly triggering or upsetting, but there is an undertone. So what is going on? The quirky morsel to observe is the circular tread of the conversation; they agree with each other to a degree. So why so tense?

Welcome to the Mehrabian rule!

These perceptions are very intricate; there is evidence to suggest decision making is often a subconscious action. Born in Iran in the brutal and tragic Armenian genocidal hangover of 1939, Professor Emeritus of Psychology Albert Mehrabian is somewhat revered for his 7-38-55 rule.

Remember the saying; the smile
doesn't match the eyes?
Instant suspicion may be induced
and a feeling of mistrust or
weariness when we get this vibe
from someone.
The more discerning we become,
the more powerful we are at
reading these messages.

Mehrabian's groundbreaking research and publications were extensive; however, his work on verbal and non-verbal messages became the tightly held tools of negotiators, FBI agencies and more recently business coaches across the globe.

Now living and teaching in California USA, the Prof's rule gave some remarkably juicy insights into human behaviour. The rule states that 7 % meaning is communicated through spoken word, 38 % through the tone of voice, and 55 % via body language. Total Liking = 7% Verbal Liking + 38% Vocal Liking + 55% Facial Liking. Mehrabian's work was all about what he called the 'silent messages' – how people communicate their intent – what they really mean non-verbally.

As Dr Nick Morman, says in Debunking The Debunkers "We get most of our clues of the emotional intent behind people's words from non-verbal sources. And when the two conflict, we believe the non-verbal every time." In other words, (pardon the pun) when I am speaking to someone and what they are saying is not matching the rest of their "output" I will rely on the non-verbal information more so.

1.

We never come to an interaction with another human without preconceived ideas. We are the result of our learning and experiences, the social cues we pick up and learn along the way are our complex resource for perceiving others, and plot twist: it is NOT always correct.

We also have body language and tone quirks that will give away what we really think or believe more so than what we are saying.

You may have read in my other articles I was blind for a time after brain surgery in 2012. Well, I can tell you this event removed 35 years of social cue learning of the non-verbal kind. Unable to observe gestures or facial expressions made it impossible to understand social nuances how I normally would. To begin with, it was frustrating, however I soon gleaned the tone of voice of others in a life-changing way. Our bodies are a work of engineering prowess. When blindness occurs often a substantial structural reorganization of the brain happens, wherein the parts of the brain typically specialized for vision are recruited for the processing of stimuli in other modalities. I know, right?

Some studies suggest that blind persons may possess "supra-normal" nonvisual sensory capabilities, as a result of either perceptual learning (Gagnon, Ismaili, Ptito, & Kupers, 2015) or the reorganization of various brain areas. For the unlearned "supra-normal" means: transcending the normal: greater than expected or usual. I know, it is pretty awesome. What you see is NOT what you always get.

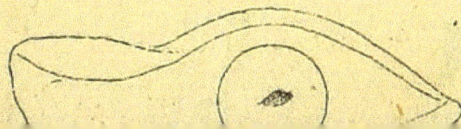

What's Your Story?

SHAPESHIFTERS, HAIRY DANCERS AND THINGS THAT GO BUMP IN THE NIGHT

BY KIRSTEN MACDONALD

Our modern-day screens are overwhelmed with creepy blood-curdling monsters.

These frequently overtly sexualised characters who morph into werewolves and vampires, sirens singing sailors to their deaths or the deep blue seas. Supernaturally charged, they have evolved from the village fireside precautionary tales and spins of old to the pop culture halls of fame.

Have you read the original Grimm brothers Fairy tales? I studied them at University, and they are not for the faint of heart. Don't even get me started on Little Red Riding Hood, because that story isn't what you think it is...

But what about the monsters lurking around the world who haven't had much love? Let's give these ghastly Villians some attention! Mind you, after you are well informed, you may understand why they are not so popular, they're not the kind you want to bring home to Mum.

The Näkki

In Finnish mythology, a Näkki (Estonian: Näkk) is a Neck. This shape-shifting water spirit usually appears in human form, residing in darkened pools, wells, docks, piers and under bridges.

Notorious for yanking down into the murky waters, it is advised for our young ones not to look into the water or lean into the depths.

Nordic mythology tells us Midsummer's night is when Näkki rises from the water to dance with people celebrating. Beautiful to look at from the front, their back is bewhiskered and uncomely.

Näkki is also called Vetehinen or Vesihiisi (water fey, see Hiisi).

Nunyunuwi The Stone Man

Known to the Cherokee nation; the Stone Man or Nunyunuwi is a shuddersome character.

A wicked cannibal, this flesh-eater prefers hunters for meals and takes on the disguise of an old man wearing a stone coat. Stories tell of his defeat and rising. There are many variations, but in all, he is dyspathetic when it comes to menstruating women. At that 'time of the month, women became powerful allies in warding off the Stone monster and his enormous hunger for human flesh.

Cuca

From Brazilian folklore, Cuca is a diabolical female monster. She is a hideous witch, with some age, and who has an alligator head. Cuca kidnaps the naughty children who won't go to sleep. She is a curmudgeonly and hellish hag that will commit evil deeds to those who don't snooze: terrifying little ones everywhere and a fearsome ally to parents all over Brazil. Close your eyes, children!

Although Cuca came from the Portuguese coca, in Tupi (an indigenous language of Brazil), Cuca means to swallow something with a single gulp.

Yikes.

Grýla

Iceland has its own Ogre, and it isn't a green loveable Dreamworks character. Grýla is a terrorizing giantess who dwells in the mountains of Iceland. She wears a prickly and hairy chin, has eyes in the back of her head and has a pet Christmas cat, a fearsome creature who eats people who don't get clothes for Christmas.

Again a tale told to frighten children (poor kids, really parents!) Gryla is known for her keen hearing, and she can smell a child from miles away. She too has a hankering for human flesh, particularly that of wicked children. She stores them away for a Christmas stew. She was so awful that in 1746 public decree prohibited parents from traumatising their kids with the tale any longer. Thank the heavens. This one is dreadful.

Draugen

Draugen is the sinister ghost of a man who died at sea terrifying Norwegian. He is behemothic, coated in seaweed, and rows in half a boat. DRaugen's trademark is an ear-piercing scream to announce his arrival, and he likes drowning sailors and those who want to fish.

Weapons do not defeat him, only a warrior can wrestle him back to his gruesome cave, and this fiendish ghoul can enter the dreams of the living along with shapeshifting and future

telling. According to the Function of the Living Dead in Medieval Norse and Celtic Literature, the mottled man is intelligent to boot; this Old Norse monster was undoubtedly worth a mention.

The Capitalismus

Finally we have the last one– the nastiest of them all– The Capitalismus.

A fire breathing monstrous beast, this one devours Brazillian rainforests with licks of fire, riding large mechanical beasts and filling it's belly with the fear of the people. A terrifying traveller, this fiend travels the globe seeking victims. Often seen as attractive and seductive, the Capitalismus cloaks itself in badges of honour and munches on sea dwellers, driving them out of their homes and lands. Particularly

shifty, this insidious trickster is very troll like and keeps dungeons of gold and silver tucked away. Not for the cowardly, this monster can only be defeated by the bravery of those who believe in equality and protecting the tribes with truth and honour.

You can read more about them here: www.britannica.com/topic/capitalism

References and important notes for our Ponderers

The Cherokee Nation is a sovereign tribal government. Upon settling in Indian Territory (present-day Oklahoma) after the Indian Removal Act, the Cherokee people established a new government in what is now the city of Tahlequah, Oklahoma. A constitution was adopted on September 6, 1839, 68 years before Oklahoma's statehood.

www.cherokee.org

The Sami are the indigenous peoples of the northern part of the Scandinavian Peninsula and much of the Kola Peninsula, and live in Sweden, Norway, Finland and Russia. It is estimated that they represent between 50,000 and 100,000.

www.iwgia.org/en/sapmi.html

The Unknown Lore of Amexem's Indigenous People: An Aboriginal Treatise

www.firstpeople.us/FP-Html-Legends/NunyunuwiTheStoneMan-Cherokee.html

nativeamericanantiquity.blogspot.com/2013/05/cherokee-witchcraft-conquering-stone.html

blogs.transparent.com/portuguese/the-legend-of-the-cuca/

guidetoiceland.is/connect-with-locals/regina/gryla-and-leppaludi-the-parents-of-the-icelandic-yule-lads

wayback.vefsafn.is/wayback/20130122160640/

icelandreview.com/icelandreview/search/news/Default.asp?ew_0_a_id=317411

www.thjodminjasafn.is/jol/adrar-vaettir/nr/2983

izi.travel/en/b530-creatures-of-norwegian-mythology/en

The function of the living dead in medieval Norse and Celtic literature: death and desire. Lewiston, New York: Edwin Mellen Press.

Nordisk familjebok Linköping University.

Old Norse: Draugr, plural draugar; modern Icelandic: draugur, Faroese: dreygur and Danish, Swedish, and Norwegian: draug) is an undead creature from Norse mythology, also called aptrganga or aptrgangr, literally "again-walker" (Icelandic: afturganga).

www.nationalgeographic.com/history/2020/04/in-brazil-indigenous-people-fighting-to-keep-children/

www.hs.fi/english/article/

TO BE HUMAN IS TO BE MUSICAL

BY KATE O'DONNELL

This year we pondered with the wonderful Allison Davies.

Safe to say this interview left the heart full and the mind is buzzing with new information and some life-changing insights.

Allison Davies has this extraordinary ability to draw on her extensive knowledge of music, the brain and all of its mechanics, and present insights in such a way, that

Growing up listening to Blues albums and Rock and Roll, Alli's first words were out of a Fats Domino song.

even the really big revelations of brains and behaviour is easy to digest and becomes common sense!

Alli is known by many as a professional music therapist. Her work with understanding the brain and Behaviours along with neurodiversity and inclusion are revelationary. Her creation of the Brain Care Cafe has also become well regarded.

Music has always impacted her life, but it wasn't until she was a neurologic music therapist that she truly understood the relationship between music and the brain.

It turns out, the information our brain gets from music, and the stimulation is far greater than you probably imagined. Relaxation music is not what you thought, and fast-paced music blaring on your road trip could encourage a lead foot and speedy driving—not joking! The mind boggles.

So what is the essential aspect people NEED to understand about music and helping the brain?

According to Allison, it is critical to reclaim our musicality and to understand that to be human is to be musical."Our brain is a musical organ.

We are all musical.
We are all driven by rhythm.
All experience melody.
We all have voice and vibration.

We need to understand this. To feel and believe that we can use music in our homes, in our classrooms, and by ourselves strategically and therapeutically and in ways that will help us and support us.

Too often, we are led to believe that we aren't musical. When it comes to music, there is no right or wrong. You can't sing out of tune unless you're singing someone else's song. YES! Shower closet rock singers unite! There is hope for us all!"

Now more than ever, anxiety is peaking, mental health, exhaustion, and dysregulation is on the rise in epic proportions. The struggle is real. Why?

"Our brains were not designed for a fast-paced, expectation dense, highly structured, modern, Western, rushed world. No humans, no brains have had this kind of environment in the last 100 years."

Alli's expert advice: We need to pull back. If we use ISO and the current COVID situation as an example.- although it's been a stressful and angsty time, with a lot of survival mode for a lot of people, simultaneously- our brain has had a break. We've been rendered choiceless and forced to pull back. Pulling back from information, back from sensory overload, back from too much socialising- this is the stuff our brain health depends on.

Allison very successfully runs the Brain Care Cafe. More than a membership, the cafe is a library of brain care strategies and a community committed to making progress on their own brain care.

Allison defines brain care as "more of what helps the brain run and less of what shuts it down."

In our daily lives, there are a lot of things we could be doing more of for our brain to function at its best. The Brain Care Cafe focuses on 12 pillar specifics that are really important for our brain. Each week Alli delivers a brain care strategy. There is an activity that will help the brain to regulate and function at its full potential. This Cafe is a library of brain care strategies. These are mostly musical based and all things we can be doing in our daily life, everyday anxiety management.

But it's not just music therapy and a string of other titles and boxes that Allison fits into. Connection is key. From her picturesque sanctuary in Tasmania, Alli shares her thoughts and processes regularly on Instagram and Facebook. The landscape is intoxicating. Nestled amongst 40mt high gumtrees, you will find her bush bath. Complete with flowers, platter and a cheeky glass of wine this is the bath Mother's Day dreams are made of! (swoon). When Ali shares a post, it feels like you are listening to a friend- and creates this beautiful space where you find yourself asking similar questions and parallel pondering!

IS THERE A DYING CAT? NO IT'S THE ART OF SINGING

BY JANELLE MCMILLAN

They will crack jokes about waking up the dead because I sound like a dying cat, then my swearing will come out perfectly.

"Why does it matter if I sound like a dying cat?" The power of music is what counts! It could be any kind of tunes from RnB, Hip Hop, Rap, Rock n Rock, Dance, Country or it might even be a bit of Opera that will take my fancy to break the silence. The black dog knows he has been beaten. As soon as I hit play, he will lay down to go to catch a couple of Z's until the time comes for him to play again. Don't take the chase of him howling to Classical, Jazz or Blues. It is not worth listening to his carry on.

The fire in my belly comes alive. My vocal chords start to wake up by doing a little dance in my throat to say, let's go and have fun.

I come alive, the noise just flows out into the room. I have just let the cat out of the bag, and everyone comes running from everywhere to see if I need something. They realise that it is only me brushing up on my singing skills.

*I don't give a sh*t about how I sound to other people.*

The music professional reckons that all singers have to be 100% perfect, but why? I can be any singer I want when I am in my world of my own and feel like a million bucks afterwards.

The power of music can break many of hours isolation without having face to face contact with friends. You will find out who are your real friends from the ones are full of shit very quickly in life, but music will always be there. It doesn't discriminate. It makes my world better because I can forget about everything that might be pissing me off. It doesn't matter if I am non-verbal or not, I have a pair of ears to listen to the words in songs and a heart to feel the messages in the songs like anyone else.

Janelle McMillan OAM is an artist and author living in Hobart, an incredible woman changing the world by helping to give her perspective about what it is like to live with Cerebral Palsy, getting around on wheels AND being a non-verbal communicator. She has a wicked sense of humour, and we welcome her contribution to Ponderings.

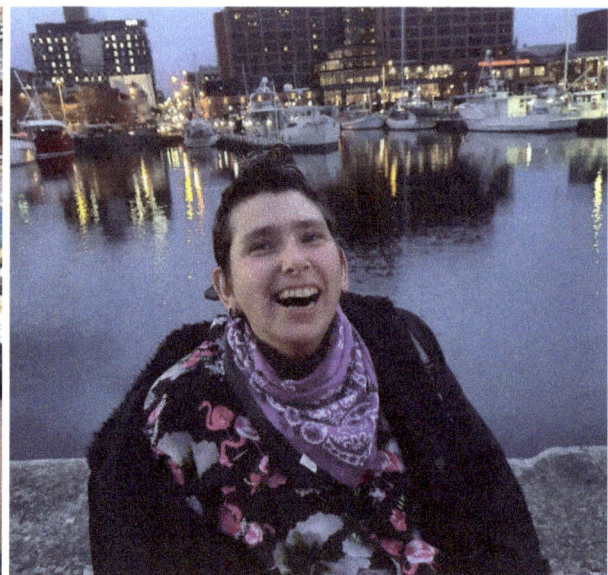

FROM MORNINGTON TO SELFRIDGES; THE TURMERIC EMPIRE STORY

BY KIRSTEN MACDONALD

For one Aussie trio, a gap in their cafe menu offering presented an opportunity and infused a story with international success.

Renwick Watts and his wife Tahli along with sister in law Sage Lamont are the team behind Golden Grind and Ponderings wanted to spill the latte on the journey from beloved ingredient to luxe bougie brand.

Turmeric; the yellow spice tantalising tastebuds and tuning in our growing love for tasty concoctions has an ancient history. With origins in Vedic culture dating back nearly 4000 years in India, Turmeric is used as a culinary spice and as a medicinal herb. Spruiked by many in the natural health sphere, Curcuma Longa has also enjoyed historical religious significance. We can vouch for that!

We ponder with Renwick Watts:

How did you begin your business?

Turmeric has been a staple in my diet from a young age. My Father originated from the West Indies, where he used Turmeric in lots of his cooking. Furthermore, my wife and Co-Founder has completed a bachelor of Dietetics and Nutrition and had heard of the benefits of Turmeric and so together, we decided to introduce the turmeric 'Golden Latte' to our menu at our family-run cafe. It was a huge success, and the business grew from there.

We noticed that the Golden latte was getting really popular in the cafe. Hence, I jumped online to see if we could buy the mix bulk/premade, and there was nothing on the internet. We also had customers, and cafe's wanting the mix, so we decided to blend in house and start supplying. But really, we were driven by the motivation to help ease inflammation for sufferers using this wonder spice!

From the decadent Miracle Turmeric Face Mask to a beyond delicious latte blend what is not to love about this brand based on passion, ethics and quality of health? Did we mention the golden spoon? It's no surprise the Aussie superfood ended up on Selfridges London shelves.

Why are you so passionate about your product, this clearly isn't just a clever idea, you really love this!

This is my favourite question. I love seeing our products help people with genuine conditions. We get a lot of testimonials whether it's our supplements helping with joint pain to our skincare helping with acne. I get such a buzz from that.

Have you got a core mission or focus?
To help prevent illness. We want to help people before they get sick so by educating them on the benefits of Eastern medicine.

What have been the highlights of running a business?
Seeing Golden Grind on the Selfridges London shelves has been a big highlight.

What have been some of the lowlights?
We have worked with some great people along the way. We have been passionate advocates for supporting local and disadvantaged people. A partnership with a disability centre doing all our packing was recently shut down, and this has been really hard for the GG team to see.

Any great lessons?
Stay true to yourself and don't give up. It's bloody hard work.

What makes your product so different from what else is out there?
The efficacy of our product. We have spent years researching and sourcing the best we can find and made products that work.

What are the main benefits of it and unusual aspects?
At the moment, it is reducing inflammation. Inflammation is the leading factor for disease globally. There are over 50 different types of Turmeric your typical shelf turmeric won't be as potent as ours.

If you could achieve one incredible goal in 2020, what would it be?
We have some really exciting NPD coming soon. I wish I could tell you more. Stay tuned...

What would you like people to know about your products they might not know?
The integrity of our products is the core focus to Golden Grind from a sustainable, organic, and quality front. We pride ourselves on delivering the best to deliver results.

Treehouse or Cubbyhouse?
I couldn't go past a treehouse. It's already bringing back such fond childhood memories. Plus I loved climbing.

Enjoy. Be Bliss. Be present. Be Golden #iamgold

QUIRKY TIDBITS FOR DINNER TABLE FACT DROPPING

BY KIRSTEN MACDONALD

Sparking interesting topics for the dinner table conversation isn't always easy. Perhaps you want to drop a complete random on someone; always a fun choice. Well, we delivered! Get your think gear around these.

Jupiter Rains Diamonds

The gassy giant some 637.41 million km away from Earth very possibly rains diamonds according to Planetary scientists Mona L. Delitsky of California Specialty Engineering and Kevin H. Baines of the University of Wisconsin-Madison.

Diamonds require carbon and pressure along with high temperatures to form. Both of which exist in Jupiter's atmosphere. Atmospheric methane gas coverts directly into diamonds which rain down into their interiors.

Drops of Jupiter has a nice ring to it, doesn't it?

Yoda's face was based on Albert Einstein

Yoda was based on Albert Einstein's face! Stuart Freeborn, an english makeup artist, based Yoda's face partly on his own and partly on Einstein's. Freeborn, had a long and wonderful career in the Star Wars franchise design and fabrication. Highly regarded, he also created the look for Ewoks and Jabba.

A Woodpeckers tongue reaches right around its skull

The tongue of a woodpecker can be extended over its entire head! The crafty forest dweller has this very long tongue in order to access ants and lava from deep crevices. With a lingua to put Gene Simmons to shame for storage, the tongue is curled around the back of the head between the skull and skin.

Elephants are the only land mammals that can't jump

When you weigh over 3 tonne, I wouldn't want to jump either. Can you imagine? Thank goodness elephants don't have wings.

Smurfs are 3 apples tall

Created by Belgian comic Pierre Culliford in 1958, the beloved Blue Smurf was exactly 3 x apples tall. Which type of apple? Not too sure. But, originally known as Les Schtroumpfs, the tribe of cute has gone the distance. I imagined them smaller did you?

The Hula Hoop was invented in Australia

A wooden hoop that Australian children twirled around their waists during gym class was patented by a toy company in the USA and given the name because of its Hawaiin dance motion a.k.a- Hula.

Hatters really were mad!

Mad as a Hatter came from hat makers using mercury to create felt. Mercury vapours were unknowingly very toxic. The toxicity caused Dementia and Erethism, aka Mad Hatter's Disease common amongst 19th Century hatmakers.

Thus "Mad as a Hatter" phrase was born. Extra fact; Lewis Carroll, the author of Alice in Wonderland, didn't use this term; his character was referred to as simply The Hatter. Mad Hatter's Disease came later. The Cheshire Cat called the March Hare and the Hatter "quite mad." However, Carroll's uncle was on the board of an asylum where many hatters and textile makers resided. Here they staged theatre plays along with tea parties. Curiouser and curiouser...

The Ponderings Story

In the beginning... Started way back in 2016, Ponderings began as a blog written by our editor Kirsten Macdonald, a brain aneurysm survivor who had a quirky, dark humoured perspective on life that resonated with people around the world. Tired of talking about herself, Kirsten recognised the platform had evolved to a space that might encompass the lives of others and tell their perhaps otherwise unheard, untold stories. A magazine was born, a news syndication and now a special edition hardcover copy.

Fast forward to 2021, a new paradigm in storytelling, Ponderings is a grassroots magazine platform and a feast for the heart and mind, seeking to inform, inspire and create reflection. Real stories and emotional intelligence combined with creating a community rewarded with a sense of connection is the guts of it. It's resonating quickly. Ponderings online magazine was born from an existential crisis and the personal forging from tragedy to triumph. Ponderings is a Magazine to spark your innate curiosity and share the stories of us. An eco-system of three dynamic layers; digital magazine + podcast, in-print anthology + App. This Anthology is our second, where each story has been curated from our most popular published pieces.

A positive space. we believe people are seeking something more, a primal need to be together in what can feel like a very separate world.

Our mission is to take you, the reader, the viewer and the listener, the witness- through a journey of tears, laughter, breathlessness and heart smiles, into a world of reflection and evaluation. A positive space, but not one that oozes positive rhetoric. Here you will find a no BS, warts and all humanity with an edge of humour that brings the tribe together. Telling each other our stories is also about developing theoretical paradigms for making sense of the world we live in. Ponderings is an expression in a discourse of a distinct mode of experiencing and thinking about the world- in simpler terms- real events showcasing interesting connections.

"The genesis of our human narrative comes from being inspired, reflecting on this inspiration and prospering from action. Bonds are formed. Our goal has succeeded; there is a sparkling thought spring for Ponderings folk to drink from in the content we wordsmith, record and present.

The most fundamental aspect of our biological origins is our social nature. 2020 showed us how instrinsically important social connection is, and how we must remember the ultimate survivor-
love x "

Kirsten Macdonald

Welcome!

PONDERINGS ANTHOLOGY REFERENCE GUIDE TO IMAGERY UNDER CREATIVE COMMONS, PUBLIC DOMAIN AND ATTRIBUTION

Ponder With Us index page
Woodblock print Katsushika Hokusai, Japanese (1760-1849)

Wherefore Art Though Drag Kween? Written by Kirsten Macdonald
All photos supplied by Art Simone

Shape Shifters, Hairy Dances and Things That Go Bump In The Night, by Kirsten Macdonald
Image: Twentieth Century Transportation, a chromolithograph by E.S Yate. Original from Library of Congress. Digitally enhanced by rawpixel

To Be Human Is to Be Musical, by Kate O'Donnell
All Images supplied by Allison Davies.

Quirky Tidbits for Dinner Table Fact Dropping, by Kirsten Macdonald
Portrait Frame by James F. Queen (Died/ 1889) design with an oval frame decorated with baby angels. Original from Library of Congress. Digitally enhanced by rawpixel.
Twentieth Century Transportation, a chromolithograph by E.S Yate. Original from Library of Congress. Digitally enhanced by rawpixel

From Mornington to Selfridges; The Tumeric Empire Story, by Kirsten Macdonald
Turmeric illustration from Les liliacées (1805) by Pierre Joseph Redouté (1759-1840). Digitally enhanced by rawpixel

A Forecast Of Charisma And Not A Plain Jane In Sight, by Kirsten Macdonald
Jane Bunn photo supplied by Jane Bunn
Bio public map. Bio Heritage Library
An upper-level weather balloon sails into the sky after release from the Cape Canaveral weather station in Florida. Original from NASA. Digitally enhanced by rawpixel
Vintage Umbrella- rawpixel

The Evolution Of Dogs, By Montanna Macdonald
Greyhound in vintage style- rawpixel
Natural paintings from the talented Flemish draughtsman Anselmus Boëtius de Boodt (1550–1632)

The Tangible Oscillation Of Us, words by Kirsten Macdonald
From Webster's New Illustrated Dictionary based on the Unabridged Dictionary of Noah Webster, Revised and edited by Edward T. Roe and Charles Leonard-Stuart, Published by syndicate Publishing Company of New York in 1911 (X-ray collage of fish, megaphone hand and shell)

Vintage Spiky Orange fish - Public Domain Heritage

Dear Grownups, by Kirsten Macdonald
Woman and child doing laundry outside black and white, Credit: Simpleinsomnia
Vintage painted flowers- yellow credit: rawpixel

The Art Of Singing by Janelle McMillan image credits: https://www.patreon.com/
stevejohnson Steve Johnson art
Janelle McMillan

The Negative Thinkers Guide to the Galaxy, Words by Kirsten Macdonald.
Discomedusae Schweibenquallen from Kuntsformen Der Natur (1904) by Ernst Kaekel-
Original from the library of Congress- enhanced by Raw Pixel detail flowers pattern vintage
Mare Humorum from the Trovelot Astronomical Drawings 1881-1882 Raw Pixel. (microscopic
view of moonlike surface)

The Blazing Heart of Community, Words by Kirsten Macdonald. Photos Kate O'Donnell and
Blazeaid Australia.

Interview with Debb Oliver-The Monkey Brush- by Renae Failla
Bindi Irwin family portrait and Mother clutching baby credit:Monkey Brush, Debb Oliver
Vintage Illustration from The Grammar of Ornament by Owen Jones

The Magic of Bees And The Beauty Of Numbers In Nature
Bees Heritage bio publish The Bio Heritage Library (Shell and Starfish and Sunflower)
A Perch of Birds- 1880 by Hector Giacomelli (1822-1904) Digitally enhanced from rawpixel's
collection of antique chromolithographics, Papillons Paris, Tolmer (ca- 1935) Bio Heritage
Library.

Five More Minutes, words by Julia Lorent
Beautiful photomechanical prints of Peony 1887-1897 by Ogawak. rawpixel

Food Glorious Food- Autism And Eating- by Kate O'Donnell
Baby on High Chair eats messily-credit: Simpleinsomnia
Children in the shoe Image from page 119 of "Harper's Young People", New York Public
Library

Exercise Myths, Activewear and Do You Want Coffee WIth That? Words by Sarah Healy
Vintage pic- Maggie Jones of Cleveland playing baseball- Public Domain.
Avion. Public Domain

The Small Town Boy Who Undressed Marilyn- Orry-Kelly an Aussie in Hollywood. By Cassidy
Krygger
Marilyn Monroe pictures- Public Domain

Puppeteer vintage public domain creative commons

How Books Save Us- more than ever… Words by Karen Brooks
Photo credit: Simpleinsomnia
The Antheneam Library- Michael D Beck

Communication Insights And Getting Grounded In A World Of Chaos, by Des Carter and Kirsten Macdonald.
Filiciane &Laubfarne from Kuntsformen Der Natur (1904) by Ernst Hackel. Original from Library of Congress. Digitally enhanced by rawpixel
Stained glass box for the Fouquet Jewelry Store by Alphonse Mari

How To Encourage A Love Of Reading In Your Children- written by Katie Moore
Image of school children reading credit- Simpleinsomnia
Photo credit- Knights Arts Challenge Detroit Charles H. Wright, Museum of African American History, Image of Katie Moore- provided by Katie Moore
Little boy with spectacles reading the "Bow Wow Book" Jan. 1924 credit: Simplinsomnia

Messages Of Hope- From Brisbane-based Poet Tom Stodulka- by Renae Failla
Image from page 66 at St Nicholas (1873)- Dodge, Mary Mapes 1830-1905, New York Scribner Information Library, Science Library University of North Carolina
Photo Tom Stodulka supplied by Tom Stodulka, Colour Image of Artwork- Tom Stoldulka
Image: Fight between a tiger and a buffalo- Henri Rosseau 1908, Cleveland Museum of Art.

I Am Too Tired To Friend, by Kate O'Donnell
Flowers from Shakespeare's garden (Lond) Cassell & Co Ltd Public Domain
Sketch of exhausted woman- The Day After 1894 by Evard Munch. Original from the MET Museum. Digitally enhanced by rawpixel

The Great Australian Pottery Revival by Renae Failla
Ceramic Art: Ancient Greek, Cyprian and Etruscan (1891) a collection of everyday tools used in the ancient times. Digitally enhanced from our original plate- rawpixel

Narcissus-Caravaggio (1594-96) edited, John William Waterhouse Echo And Narcissus
Giovanni Antonio Boltraffio, Narcissus, probably about 1500, London, National Gallery
Jan Roos - Narcissus at the Spring

Secret Messages by Kirsten Macdonald
Vintage key illustration Raw Pixel Creative Commons Public Domain, Romano Guidotti
PUBLIC DOMAIN 2017
Erpétologie générale, ou, Histoire naturelle complète des reptiles
Paris :Roret,1834-1854

www.ingramcontent.com/pod-product-compliance
Lightning Source LLC
Chambersburg PA
CBHW040315100426
42811CB00012B/1447